The Bathtub Is Overflowing but I Feel Drained

Lysa TerKeurst

HARVEST HOUSE PUBLISHERS

EUGENE, OREGON

Cover by Garborg Design Works, Minneapolis, Minnesota

Cover photos © sylvanworks/iStockphoto; benoitb/iStockphoto; Emrah Turudu/iStockphoto

THE BATHTUB IS OVERFLOWING BUT I FEEL DRAINED
Copyright © 2006 by Lysa TerKeurst
Published by Harvest House Publishers
Eugene, Oregon 97402
www.harvesthousepublishers.com

Library of Congress Cataloging-in-Publication Data

TerKeurst, Lysa.
   The bathtub is overflowing but I feel drained / Lysa TerKeurst.
      p. cm.
   ISBN-13: 978-0-7369-1866-4 (pbk.)
   ISBN-10: 0-7369-1866-3 (pbk.)
   Product # 6918664
   1. Mothers—Religious life. 2. Motherhood—Religious aspects—Christianity. I. Title.
   BV4529.18.T44 2006
   248.8'431—dc22   2006001343

Printed in the United States of America

06 07 08 09 10 11 12 13 14 / VP-KB / 10 9 8 7 6 5 4 3 2 1

I lovingly dedicate this book to the little girl who ate my mud pies and cleaned my room for a penny... my sister, Angee Dixon.

What an amazing woman and mother you have become.

Acknowledgments

To my husband, Art...you are the love of my life.

To the five people who make it possible for me to be called that glorious title of Mommy:

> Jackson...the day you came home and told me you led your friend to Christ is one I'll treasure forever.

> Hope...the day you shared with me your profound thoughts on friendship quirks is one I'll treasure forever.

> Mark...the day you sat me down and listed all the reasons you appreciate me still brings tears to my eyes and is one I'll treasure forever.

> Ashley...the day you told me you were secretly fasting for a hurting family is one I'll treasure forever.

> Brooke...the day you promised to pray for my every speaking engagement is one I'll treasure forever. And yes, my sweet girl... to answer the question you ask me often...I will be your mommy forever.

To Marybeth Whalen...you are more than a friend; you are a gift from God. Thank you for helping make the Bible studies in this book possible.

To Kim Moore and the staff at Harvest House...without you these words would be stuck in a file somewhere. Thank you for believing they were worth publishing.

To Lydia Lewis...you amaze me in the incredible ways you have supported my ministry and loved me like one of your own.

To LeAnn Rice, Renee Swope, and Genia Rogers...I would not want to do ministry without you.

To all the Proverbs 31 Ministry staff, speaking team, board members, and supporters...thank you for standing with me as we impact this world for Christ.

Contents

A Refilled Heart

1

Who Are These People Calling Me Mom?

*The world is full of women blindsided
by the unceasing demands of
motherhood, still flabbergasted by how
a job can be terrific and torturous.*

Anna Quindlen

I sank down deep into the bubbles, my body tired and sore. I thought I was going to love motherhood and embrace it with great and unabashed joy. But that was not at all how I was feeling, especially today. What was wrong with me? Something had better kick in soon as I was about to start the whole adventure over again with baby number two. She'd be arriving in five short weeks.

Tears trickled down my cheeks as I recalled the day's events. I'd taken my 14-month-old daughter to a department store sale to stock up on things I needed for the new baby. I was well equipped for our trip with a stroller, snacks in little baggies, sippie cups full of her favorite beverages, and toys to keep her entertained. But she was not impressed with any of my offerings once we got to the store. She became obsessed with the cash register manuals behind the checkout counter.

She discovered them the first time she wiggled from the restraints holding her in the stroller. As she wandered behind the counter, the sales lady, who got my attention in a stern voice that made me feel incapable and irresponsible, asked me to please keep my daughter from wandering. I picked up Hope and put her back in the stroller. She was very unhappy, to say the least. I tried to appease her with several things from the diaper bag. When nothing was working, I pulled out my ultimate weapon, the bottle. I'd promised myself I'd only use this in a dire circumstance as we'd been trying to wean her before the new baby came. But it brought me the peace and cooperation I needed to keep on shopping.

No sooner had I started comparing prices again when I spotted Hope's bottle on the ground and the stroller empty. About this time I heard a loud crash coming from behind the register with the irritated salesclerk and the cash register manuals. I flew behind the counter just as stern woman was about to open her mouth. I held up my hand as if to say "Nothing you are about to say could make me feel any more embarrassed than I already am."

I also felt condemning stares from other customers. I was sure they were all wondering why I couldn't keep my daughter under control and would love to give volumes of advice if only I'd ask. I knew this is what they were thinking because B.K. (before kids) I used to see unruly children and have these same thoughts. *My children would never act that way! That poor mother needs some advice from me.* Oh, how our judgments come back to haunt us.

I picked Hope up, put her face where she had to look squarely into my eyes and in the harshest voice I could whisper said, "Mommy told you no. Do not get out of your stroller. Do not touch the books. Do not wander off. Do you understand NO!?!" Just as I finished my correction, she reared her head back, threw it toward my head, and bit me! She sunk her sharp little teeth right into my cheek. I could not believe what was happening. All I knew is that I had to get out of that store and away from my vampire child.

I tucked Hope, still screaming for the manuals, under one arm, picked the stroller up and tucked it under my other arm, and waddled out of the store. By the time I reached my car, we were a tangled mess of baby gear and tears. I drove straight to my husband's restaurant, marched in holding Hope at arm's length, and instructed him to put her in the baby backpack as she was staying with him for the remainder of the day. When he inquired about the bleeding gash on my face, all I could say was, "This is exactly the reason I can't have her with me right now."

I drove home and drew a hot bath, but not even Calgon could take me away. As I lay my head back against the tub's edge, I kept thinking about what a failure I was. Through my tears I stared at the water pouring out of the tub's faucet. I want to offer what this water offers to everyone who releases it from the faucet. It brings warmth and comfort. It fills a space without leaving any gaps. It is clean and able to wash away the yuck of life. It has a vast supply of its offering. It is pure and without hidden or harsh elements. It fulfills the purpose for which it was made.

I let the water run until the tub could not contain another drop. Even at my slightest movement, the water sloshed about and overflowed onto the floor. There was such a stark difference between my soul and the water in the tub. I thought to myself, "The tub is overflowing, but I am completely drained."

Most moms can relate to this feeling. That's why I wrote this book. It's not a parenting book. It's not a how-to-be-the-best-mom-ever book. It's not a one-size-fits-all advice book. It's a gut-honest look at motherhood. Through all the pushes and pulls, stresses and strains, and triumphs and failures there are perspectives I have found to be encouraging and even transforming. I have discovered that if I can change the way I think about something, I can change the way I react to it. If I change the way I react, I can change the way I define myself as a mother. I don't have to be defined as one barely hanging on in survival mode. I can be a mom who thrives and lives and loves the great adventure I've been called to.

So whether you are pushing a stroller while a toddler squirms about or pushing a hole in the floorboard of your car while your teen learns to drive, join me for a few weeks and let's do life together. Keep your Bible handy and your heart open. I can't promise you'll know the answer to every motherhood question after we finish this book, but I can promise you'll look at your role with a refilled heart, a refueled approach, a renewed perspective, and a soul that feels refreshed.

I have been through lots more tub days since those early years with Hope. I now have five kids. Me! The woman who could barely handle one child, and now I have five. I am not a perfect mom, but I have learned to embrace motherhood with a great sense of joy. It is a calling. I must always keep in mind that how I handle this calling will shape the generations that come after me. What a sobering and yet thrilling thought. The traditions I start with my children will be carried on. The foundations I build with my children will be built upon. The morals, values, and spiritual disciplines I teach will shape and mold my children, grandchildren, great-grandchildren, and others I won't ever meet.

My family will be my greatest legacy. More than the things I accomplish. More than the home I make warm and lovely. More than the people's lives I impact. More than anything else I am known for. If I fulfill the calling of being a godly wife and mother, then I will be satisfied.

Since you'll be hearing a lot about those I love most in this book, I thought I should give you a brief introduction. Art is my handsome husband who loves to hunt, fish, and scuba dive. He and the boys spend hours working on our land using dangerous guy things such as chainsaws, tractors, and industrial mowers. Art calls himself a professional chicken flipper because he works for Chick-fil-A, home of the yummiest chicken sandwiches and sweet tea. (Knowing where he works might give you a better visual of what Art was doing when I brought Hope in on the "wounded face" day. He was working the register, taking people's orders and, I'm sure, doing a lot of explaining as to why he had a baby strapped to him.)

Our sons, Jackson and Mark, were adopted several years ago from Liberia, Africa. They are amazing boys. How God blessed our lives with Jackson and Mark is a beautiful story of obedience and blessing. I wrote several chapters about it in my last book, *What Happens When Women Walk in Faith,* so I won't go into it here.

Jackson is our oldest son. He loves Chinese food, country music, and basketball. He has big goals and would like to be a businessman or a chef. Whatever he does, he's sure to be successful. He is teaching me a lot about cool music, hip sayings, and the latest trends for teens. Jackson loves the Lord and loves being a leader in his youth group.

Mark loves anything that has crushed red pepper mixed in it, especially hot wings and spicy rice. He is a talented soccer player and holds the record for the largest fish caught in our pond by any family member. He has a very tender heart and wants to be a missionary. Maybe Jackson will make enough money to support his brother on the mission field one day.

Hope is our oldest daughter. She is very organized and responsible. She still loves manuals of all kinds, which is a great asset to a mother who is emotionally allergic to instruction booklets. She is very determined and would like to be a teacher or the president of the United States...whichever makes more money.

Ashley is only a year younger than her big sister. She is a sweet-spirited child who loves math and who spends hours each week practicing gymnastics. She has her dad's athletic ability and is always giving the other family members dance moves. She would like to open an orthodontic practice with her best friend one day.

Brooke is the baby of the family and proud of it. She is a ray of sunshine everywhere she goes. She is quite the little dresser and loves to give advice to Mommy if I ever stray from looking fashionable. When I asked Brooke what she wanted to be when she grows up, she threw her head back and with a smile simply said, "Beautiful."

Well, now that you know a little more about my family, I hope it makes your journey through this book more meaningful. We are an everyday family. I am an everyday mom. But I have learned the amazing blessings that come from saying yes to doing life God's way, and I can't wait to share them with you. I pray this book is just the adventure your soul needs to look at motherhood with more joy than ever before.

Refresh My Soul

Read Psalm 23:3.

Do you need to be restored?

Changing your perspective on motherhood will not happen in one day. There will not be a moment when you feel a magical transformation occur. Instead, you will learn over the course of this book that you can make little decisions each day that will transform your motherhood experience.

Each decision will build on itself. Bit by bit you will find that right decisions lead to hope, and hope leads to transformation. Second Peter 1:5-7 says, "Make every effort to add to your faith goodness; and to your goodness, knowledge; and to knowledge, self-control; and to self-control, perseverance; and to persever-ance, godliness; and to godliness, brotherly kindness; and to brotherly kindness, love." Just as the virtues mentioned in this verse build on themselves, so one good choice leads to another good choice and results in change in your life.

You just have to take one step at a time. One right attitude. One good decision. One perspective change. These little changes will lead to big results.

Above all, be patient with yourself and with God through this process. Don't expect instant gratification—that is not the way He works.

Take some time to write down what you would like to have happen in your life as a result of reading this book. What are your expectations and hopes? What are some changes right now that you already know you would like to make in your motherhood?

Be open to God's leading and dependent on His Word, and you will see great things happen as a result—in your motherhood and in your life. My prayer for you is that you will enjoy the journey this book will take you on, and that you and your children will be changed forever as a result of this experience.

2

I'm the Worst Mom Ever

Write injuries in dust, benefits in marble.

BENJAMIN FRANKLIN

I was supposed to be going on a fun scrapbooking retreat for the weekend. My friends left on Thursday and called to tell me what a great time they were having. How I wanted to be there with them! But Art had to be out of town and the kids needed me at home. I felt pulled in a thousand directions. Ashley wanted me to watch her at gymnastics. Hope wanted to be dropped off at a friend's house. Brooke wanted a friend to come over, and the boys had to be taken to soccer practice.

It's not that I didn't want to be with the kids. I love my children and love spending time with them. It's just that I was tired. I was serving from the dregs of my bucket rather than the overflow. I had looked forward to the weekend with my friends laughing, eating out, and catching up on putting the family pictures in albums.

On a scale from one to ten, my stress level hovered around a seven. I wanted to take time to be with the Lord and allow His Word to bathe my parched soul and bring my stress back to a manageable level, but constant time crunches kept me distracted. Feeling tired and underappreciated, I should have known I was setting myself up for failure.

On Saturday morning I got up at 5:00 to take the boys and several of their friends to an out of town soccer game. I wouldn't be able to stay at the game because I had to rush back to get Ashley to the gym and then run home to clean the house. Art would be home that night by dinnertime, and the house needed some serious attention before his arrival.

I was out the door by 5:45 with four boys and Ashley in tow. About halfway to the soccer game, the kids brought it to my attention that nobody had eaten breakfast. My stress level jumped to a nine and voices of accusation started dancing in my head. *What kind of mom sends her kids to play soccer with no food in their bellies? What would the boys' friends tell their parents? "I could have played really well today, except Mrs. TerKeurst didn't feed us."*

We didn't have time to stop before dropping the boys off at the field, but they would have a warm-up time before the game started, which would give me time to zip through a drive-through and bring food back to them. Maybe they could down a few bites of a biscuit between the end of warm-ups and the start of the game. So I dropped the boys off and then Ashley and I went to find biscuits.

When I got to the window to pick up my food, I was surprised by the enormous size of our drinks. The cups were so large they wouldn't fit in my car's cup holders. However, there was no time to switch them out for a smaller size, so I paid for our order and drove off. I told Ashley to please hold on to the drinks as they would tip easily if we weren't careful.

I had no sooner turned out of the parking lot when I hit a pothole, and what seemed like gallons of tea dumped onto the floor of my car. In a frustrated huff I raised my voice. "Ashley, I told you to hold on to those drinks!" My stress level jumped past a ten when Ashley snapped back at me, "Mom, YOU just made me spill the drinks!"

I don't know from what dark, unbridled corner of my heart my next response came. It must have been lurking there for a while just waiting to pop out and horrify me. Me, the mom who had taken such pride that she'd never cussed at her kids. Me, the Proverbs 31 woman with a ministry teaching women the importance of using kind words to correct her children. Me, the woman who writes books and speaks to thousands and can be heard on the radio teaching about godliness. Me, the woman who teaches Bible studies whipped my head around to my daughter and yelled, "Shut up and eat your d*** biscuit." And I wasn't talking about the little houses beavers make. No, there it was in broad daylight....a cuss word that spilled from my lips.

The same lips that read bedtime stories, say nighttime prayers, and tenderly kiss my children good night. The same lips that tell others about Jesus. The same lips that sing God's praises. Oh, the horror I felt. I think Ashley was more shocked that I said "shut up" as she'd never heard the other word before. But I still felt like the worst mom in the world.

After a few moments of silence, I apologized. We drove to the soccer game, and while Ashley delivered her brothers' biscuits I called a friend. With tears in my eyes, I recounted the morning's events. Then, before I told her the dreaded sentence, I warned her, "You are going to think I'm the worst mom ever. You're just not going to believe what I did!" I repeated this warning statement several times just to make sure she was prepared for the horror that was coming.

Then I whispered what I'd yelled at Ashley...beaver home and all.

"That's it? That's it? That's what you are so upset about? Apologize to her, ask God for forgiveness, and get over it. So you had a hard morning. Stop letting Satan get the best of you and ask God to give you a new attitude."

What? She didn't condemn me? She didn't agree that I'm the worst mom ever? She didn't hop in her van, speed my way, and stone me? What freedom. What a gift of grace. What a friend!

I bowed my head and asked God to protect Ashley's heart from the dart I shot at her, and I asked Him to wipe this whole event from her mind. I asked God to forgive me, not just for my ugly words, but most of all for getting too busy to spend time with Him.

As I mopped up my van overflowing with tea, I realized that I'd been living life backward that week. I was letting my to-do list overflow while withholding my time with the Lord. When what I should have done is let my time with the Lord overflow while withholding my to-do list.

It's a mistake I think a lot of us moms make. We're a slave to the tyranny of the urgent. But how can we continue to pour out if we aren't being filled back up on a daily basis? The flood of demands will consume us if we don't take the time to let God right our perspective, reduce our stress level, and whisper His tender truths of love in our ear.

Have you ever had a "worst mom ever" day? Take heart, so have we all. Take my friend's advice. Apologize to your children. Ask God for forgiveness. Get over it and stop letting Satan drag you down. Spend time with the Lord getting a new attitude, and He'll help you leave the dams to the beavers!

Refresh My Soul

Read Psalm 103:1-4.

Before stating that God forgives his sins, David (the author of this psalm), praises God first. Write some praises for God here.

In verse 2, what does David mean by "forget not all his benefits"?

List the verbs that are found in verses 3-5.

What does God forgive?

What does God heal?

What does God redeem?

What does God crown you with?

What does God satisfy your desires with?

When He does all of this, verse 5 ends by saying that your "youth is renewed like the eagle's." In other words, life, energy, and vitality return to your spirit.

Read Psalm 103:8-13.

How is God's love for you described?

What does God do with our sins?

If God removes our sins, then why do we allow Satan to beat us up for them? Let God remove your sin and leave it with Him. Satan can't beat us up with sin that we've let God truly have. Only when we hold on to it can Satan use it against us. Learn what God wants to teach you about this sin in your heart and then let it go.

Does fearing God mean an "afraid of Him" fear? No, fearing God is a healthy respect and reverence of Him. How do you show this to the Lord?

We often think of God as big and powerful and mighty. But in this psalm it is very clear that His tender compassion is there for us as well. How do you show your own children compassion?

Read back through what you've written about your compassion for your children and write how God is compassionate with you.

Verses 17-18 tell us the Lord's love is with whom?

Does the word "perfect" ever appear in those verses?

Whose righteousness will be with your children and your children's children?

Righteousness is a big religious word that can be broken down in a simple form by substituting "right choices that honor God." God will give you the ability to make right choices that honor Him if you will ask Him for that. He will do the same for your children. Because our children will model our behavior, we want to make right choices that honor God. But even when we mess up, we can model right behavior to our children by pointing back to God's forgiveness, healing, and restoration.

Just as this psalm started out with praise, it ends with praise as well. Praise God for how He has touched your heart today.

3

No More Yuckies

Sow a thought, you reap an act;
sow an act, you reap a habit; sow
a habit, you reap character; sow a
character, you reap a destiny.

AUTHOR UNKNOWN

Many things amaze me about being a mom, especially a mom's ability to understand what the cry of her child means. Just the pitch and sound speak volumes to a mother's heart. A whine means I'm tired. A whimper means I'm frustrated. A shrill means I'm excited. A scream means I'm scared. A deep-from-the-gut cry means I'm hurt. A muffled, moaning cry means I'm sick.

So when I heard the moaning cry coming from my youngest, Brooke, I knew a long night was ahead of us. A stomach bug had caused her to get sick all over her bed, her carpet, her stuffed animals, and even her nightstand. While I consoled my crying child, I took inventory of the mess and started to feel completely overwhelmed. I asked Art if I could get his wet/dry shop vac from the garage. Maybe I could just suck everything clean, throw the vacuum away, and get a new one tomorrow. I admit this plan seemed a bit wasteful, but it was completely justifiable in my opinion. Art didn't think my idea would work. Bummer.

My husband very graciously offered to work on the room while I took our daughter downstairs to get her cleaned up. No sooner had I gotten Brooke clean and tucked into a pallet on my floor when the yuckies struck again. This time she required a bath. As soon as I got her cleaned up she got sick again. So I decided the two of us had better stay in the bathroom together. I held her and tried to console her with a wet cloth on her forehead and gentle strokes of comfort on her back.

With tears in her eyes she looked up at me and said, "Mommy, I've prayed God would make me stop throwing up, but He's not answering my prayer."

"Oh, sweetheart," I softly replied. "God wants all the yuckies to get out of your tummy so your body can be healthy again. He'll help you stop throwing up as soon as the yuckies are gone. Why don't we pray together right now."

With her little raspy voice she started. "Lord, thank You for this most wonderful day. Please help me to stop being sick. But most of all, thank You for this most wonderful day."

I was stunned. With tears in my eyes I thought, *I want to be just like her when I grow up.* In the middle of life's yuck I want to still be able to see God's goodness and thank Him for each wonderful day. Instead, I often get caught up in the emotional waves of life's ups and downs and lose sight of God's goodness.

Is it really possible to operate in God's peace and rest in His goodness despite the circumstances that come our way? Philippians 4:4-7 says,

> Rejoice in the Lord always. I will say it again: Rejoice! Let your gentleness be evident to all. The Lord is near. Do not be anxious about anything, but in everything, by prayer and petition, with thanksgiving, present your requests to God. And the peace of God, which transcends all understanding, will guard your hearts and minds in Christ Jesus.

These verses outline steps to walking in God's peace.

Rejoice

To rejoice means to verbalize your pleasure. God delights in our pleasure, but verbalizing our pleasure in times of stress is often exactly the opposite of what we feel like doing. We want to verbalize our complaints, our frustration, and our anxiety. But we must ask ourselves what good does this ever bring about? Does any good ever come about when we rant and rave about our circumstances? For me, ranting and raving just heaps more frustration on the situation and leaves me feeling even more drained.

If, however, I choose to rejoice, not in my circumstances, but in the Lord's ability to handle what I can't, I invite God's peace to invade that moment. When I simply say, "Lord, You are good even when my circumstances are not. Thank You for this day. This is Your day. Help me walk in it in a manner that proclaims Your presence in my life." Making this statement brings the next part of Philippians 4:5 to life: "Let your gentleness be evident to all."

Be Gentle

When we think about the word "gentle," we think about the way a butterfly lands on a flower's petal, the way a quiet breeze passes by our face, or the way a mother touches a newborn. Gentleness in our life is evidence that God's Spirit has landed on us, His breath of new life has passed through us, and the depth of our soul has been touched by Him. When we are gentle even when life is harsh, we show that God is real. People meet the reality of God in us when our spirit reflects His character rather than our natural reactions.

Trust me, this is a practiced discipline for me. I'm not naturally a gentle person, but the more I make the choice to let God's Spirit reign in me, the more the practice of being gentle becomes possible for me. Not that I just pull myself up by the bootstraps and will gentleness to ooze from my being. No, I ask God to diffuse my emotional response and give me His response. This is my declaration that the next part of Philippians 4:5 is true: "The Lord is near."

Know that He Is Near

Having a stomach bug is about as low as Brooke could imagine her life being. She is unaware of much of the stresses of life, but being that sick was bad. I was so touched by her reaction because the first thing she did was to call on the Lord. She knew He would be able to help her. She knew He would be available. She knew His touch would be powerful. She knew He would be near.

Do we really know God is near? To answer this question for myself, I have to ask, "What is my first reaction when the yuckies of life hit? Is it to get mad or is it to get motivated to press in to God?" When my children have a need, they come to me and ask because they know I have the ability to help them. When I come to God, I not only say I believe He is near, but I also say I believe in His ability to help me. Because I know He can help me in any and every situation, I don't have to be anxious about anything...any big thing, any small thing, anything at all.

Pray

"Do not be anxious about anything, but in everything, by prayer and petition, with thanksgiving, present your requests to God. And the peace of God, which transcends all understanding, will guard your hearts and minds in Christ Jesus" (Philippians 4:6-7).

These verses say it all. Prayer is powerful, but prayer *with* thanksgiving is key. When we present our requests to God through thankful prayers, God's peace will fill us and protect us. Our heart contains our emotions and our mind contains our thoughts. If we want our emotions and thoughts to come under the authority of God, we must tap into His peace. It will guard us from being swept away, discouraged, and overwhelmed. Satan loves to sweep our thoughts and emotions away in a sea of troubles, but his schemes are thwarted the minute we call on the power of the Lord.

Just as a mom knows the cries of her child, God knows our cries as well. He knows when we are tired and He will give us rest. He knows when we are frustrated and He will give us relief. He knows when we are excited and He will share in our joy. He knows when we are scared and He will calm our fear. He knows when we are sick and He will give us comfort. He is a tender Father with a gentle touch.

Thank You, God, for this most wonderful day. God, will You rid my heart of the yuckies of doubt, discouragement, and stress and help me be filled with You? But most of all, thank You for this most wonderful day.

Refresh My Soul

Read Psalm 139:23-24 and then write it here:

David verbalized to God just before verse 23 extreme words against those who were against God. David was honest with God about the things that troubled him. Have you been honest with God about the things troubling you? Write one thing here that has been troubling you and be honest with God about your feelings.

After he verbalized his honest feelings, David asked God to reveal any wrong motives behind his strong statements. It's important to understand that we can't change other people, and often we can't change the circumstances that come our way, but we can ask God to change us. Ask God to allow you to see things and people from His perspective…to lead you to the truth. It is important to look at the truth about ourselves. God wants to get the yuckies out of our hearts every day. Name one yuckie you need to be rid of today.

Sometimes we are afraid to get too close to people for fear they will discover things they don't like. But we don't have to be afraid of God knowing our deepest thoughts and feelings. He already knows us and loves us right where we're at. Read Psalm 139:1-6. Write verses 5-6 here:

Read Psalm 139:7-10. God loves us right where we are, but He loves us too much to leave us there. He wants us to grow and develop our character to match our calling. Read James 1:2-4. God does not mean for us to find joy in the trials, but rather find joy in what the trials can develop in us.

What does the testing of your faith develop?

When we learn to persevere, what do we gain?

Complete and not lacking in anything means filled up completely. In other words, when we face trials that drain us, we can take comfort in knowing that God will refresh and refill us. God uses the trials to bring us face-to-face with the yuckies in our heart that need to be dealt with. But He doesn't leave us in that hard place. If we allow Him to work in our heart, He'll fill the empty place up with His joy.

Read Psalm 139:13-16 and write out the parts of these verses that are most precious and meaningful to you.

God doesn't define you by any yuck in your heart. He defines you as a wonderfully treasured child that He perfectly made. Read Psalm 139:17-18 and record your thoughts here:

4

A Mom's Greatest Fear

*Only those are fit to live who do not
fear to die. And none are fit to die who
have shrunk from the joy of life and
the duty of life. Both life and death are
parts of the same great adventure.*

THEODORE ROOSEVELT

A father's greatest fear is usually that he won't be able to provide for his family. A mom's greatest fear is typically that something will happen to one of her children. Fear is a funny thing. It sometimes provides healthy caution, but more times than not it seems to produce undue stress and anxiety regarding things over which we have little to no control.

The Bible has a lot to say about fear. According to one Bible text search, "fear not," or the equivalent to that, is said 365 times. Let's see, how many days of the year are there? Well, that means we have a verse to hang on to every day of the year.

Here are some of my favorite verses on fear:

So do not fear, for I am with you; do not be dismayed, for I am your God. I will strengthen you and help you; I will uphold you with my righteous right hand (Isaiah 41:10).

Fear not, for I have redeemed you; I have summoned you by name; you are mine. When you pass through the waters, I will be with you; and when you pass through the rivers, they will not sweep over you. When you walk through the fire, you will not be burned; the flames will not set you ablaze. For I am the LORD, your God, the Holy One of Israel, your Savior (Isaiah 43:1-3).

The LORD is my light and my salvation—whom shall I fear? The LORD is the stronghold of my life—of whom shall I be afraid? (Psalm 27:1).

One day I was fretting over having allowed one of my children to go to the lake with another family. I totally trust this other family, and I had no real reasons to feel anxious, but this gnawing feeling of what-if seemed to be my constant companion. I kept having little flashes of her getting injured or worse. I went to Art and asked if by any chance he was having these same feelings. He simply said no.

I couldn't help but dig a little deeper and question him further. "You mean, you haven't thought about any what-if scenarios regarding our daughter's safety today?"

"No, I really haven't," he calmly replied.

"You've got to be kidding," I said, not believing that he could go a whole afternoon and never have just one of my same fearful thoughts. My curiosity piqued, I just had to ask more questions. "Do you ever get scared when the kids ride in cars with other people? I mean, do you ever see them ride off and lift up urgent pleas for their safety? Or what about when the boys went on that missions trip this summer? Were your senses on high alert until they were once again safe under our roof? What about when the girls flew to see their grandmother this summer? Did any fearful thoughts of past plane crashes flash through your mind? What about all the times I fly to speaking engagements? Are you fearful for my safety?"

He simply said, "Of course I want you all to be safe, and of course I pray for that. But afraid? No, I can't say I'm afraid."

Suddenly, a profound thought hit me. I think this is why I am so mentally spent by the end of the day. My mind is constantly on the go where my kids are concerned. Most things are small, everyday concerns, such as: Did they brush their teeth? Are they cold? Did they have enough breakfast? Did they study their spelling words? But then I have flashes of fear that pierce my heart and make my pulse quicken. Mostly this happens when I hear of bad things happening to other children. A terrible car accident, a brain tumor, a heart defect, a drowning, a child choking—this list of what-if's goes on and on. No wonder I'm so tired!

I studied my husband quizzically and wondered how he could live above the fear of possible tragedy. Then the perfect analogy came to me to help him understand how exhausting these fears can be. "Honey, I think about the well-being of our kids and ponder their health and safety as much as you think about sex! Does that help shed light on how much this consumes my mental energy?" He just smiled and shook his head.

It's okay for us moms to be protective over our children and watch out for their well-being. That's one of the most important aspects of our job. But it's not okay for the fear of the unknown to paralyze us and stifle our kids in the process. The reality is that God has assigned a certain number of days to our children, and nothing we do or don't do will add to that number. "Who of you by worrying can add a single hour to his life?" (Matthew 6:27).

I do not speak of this topic lightly. I know that bad things really do sometimes happen to children. When I was 18 years old, my mom gave birth to my beautiful sister, Haley. Because of our vast age difference, she was more like my child than my sister. I loved Haley so deeply and completely. But tragedy struck when she was only 16 months old. She survived a liver transplant, but complications set in during a routine follow-up surgery. Despite all our pleas for the Lord to spare her, His answer was no. Haley passed away.

I was certain that after my family walked through a tragedy of this magnitude it could never happen to us again. But when my Ashley was only six weeks old, she became gravely ill. My husband and I heard words from a doctor that no parent ever wants to hear: "We aren't sure she can make it through the surgery. You have five minutes to tell her goodbye." Though my voice was paralyzed and silent, my soul screamed out, "Nooooo, You cannot take her. I will not let You take her." How do you tell a lifetime of dreams all wrapped up in one child goodbye?

As they wheeled her away, I collapsed into my husband's arms. He gently led me out to the parking lot of the hospital. Outside, he cupped my face in his hands and asked me who Ashley really belonged to. Whose child is she really? With each of his questions, I kept saying she was my child. Through his own tears, he kept asking these same questions until, finally, I answered him with the truth. "She is God's child."

"That's right. She is God's child. He gave her to us, and if He chooses, He might take her. But whether He leaves or takes her, we have to stand here today and say we love Him no matter what. We're not saying we love what He might allow to happen, but we must love God for who He is, not what He does." I knew Art was right, but I could not stand the thought of losing my daughter. At the same time, I couldn't stand the thought of letting my soul become vulnerable to walking away from God if His answer was no. I had walked away from God when we lost Haley, and it was the darkest time of my life. I could not do that again.

So in the middle of our tears and pain, Art and I mentally lifted up our daughter and released her back to God. Though my tears did not cease, the panic in my heart did. I felt the most amazing peace wash over me and fill up every hurting crevice in my soul.

Ashley's crisis ended differently than Haley's. God's answer was to leave her with us and she was healed. Why did God spare Ashley and take Haley? I'll never know. But the motherhood lesson I learned that day in the parking lot will stay with me forever. When I fear for my children, I have to relive this exercise. I have to go back to that parking lot and lift my children up to God. I have to state that they are His first and foremost. I have to proclaim my love for God no matter what. Yes, I ask for them to be kept safe. Yes, I believe in the power and provision of prayer. But I have to realize that I cannot control my children's safety. Not by my prayers, not by my worries, and certainly not by my fears.

Maybe you have never walked through this exercise. Close your eyes and stand in that parking lot with me. Lift each of your children up to the Lord. Pray for their protection and provision. Tell Him that you trust Him. But let the deepest cry of your heart be for the courage to tell God you will love Him no matter what.

Refresh My Soul

Read Psalm 27:1; 34:4; 46:1-2.

Do you remember the first time your child ever told you he or she was afraid? I can remember when each of my girls went from confident, fearless toddlers to fearful, shy preschoolers. They began to be aware of things that could harm them. Loud noises, the dark, and monsters under the bed suddenly became a part of their world. While they knew Mommy and Daddy could protect them, and I taught them to pray when they were scared, fear was still a part of their lives.

I am not unlike my children where fear is concerned. While I may not be afraid of monsters under the bed, I do allow other fears to spring up in my life. Someone once told me that FEAR is "False Expectations Appearing Real." I fear childhood illnesses, parenting failures, and the future. I allow the unknown to overtake my life and cloud my judgment. By doing this, I allow these what-if scenarios to take on larger-than-life proportions.

When this happens, I must stop this train of thought and make one of two choices: react to the fear or turn to the Lord. When I react to the fear, I make irrational decisions that generally go against who God has called me to be. What I do out of fear never accomplishes God's purposes for me. I have learned that God does not honor decisions in my life that are a result of my thinking, "Well, I need to do _____ because I am afraid of _____."

These are the moments in which I must stop going down that path, confess my fears, and offer them up to God. By doing this, I can break free from fear and take action according to His divine direction.

If you are dealing with fear today, make the choice to turn toward God and not give in to the fear. Write your choice here.

Identify the fears you are facing right now. Write down a prayer to the Lord about these fears. Confess them to Him and ask Him to help you do battle with fear in your life.

Here's a prayer I pray often:

Dear Lord, please help me to make the right choice when fear threatens to invade my life. Help me not to react to fear, but to turn to You. Thank You, Lord, for being the stronghold of my life.

Are you allowing false expectations to appear real in your life?

Are there chronic fears that Satan uses to distract you from accomplishing God's purpose for you?

Learn to recognize when fear is running away with you and don't go down that path.

If you are struggling with fear, copy Psalm 27:1 on an index card and post it somewhere that is visible throughout your day. Do a word study using your Bible concordance to find other verses that speak to your heart about fear. I will leave you with one I like:

> In righteousness you will be established: tyranny will be far from you; you will have nothing to fear. Terror will be far removed; it will not come near you (Isaiah 54:14).

5

A Mom's Greatest Joy

I have no greater joy than to hear that
my children are walking in the truth.

3 JOHN 4

It had been a disappointing week for my kids. Brooke had hoped for a solo in the school play and did not get it. Mark and Jackson's basketball team lost a big game. Ashley did not do as well as she had hoped at a gymnastics meet. Hope scored low on a test in a subject she usually did well in. Though the events were small in the grand scheme of life, they were big to my kids in the frame of that week. They got over the disappointment quickly, but as a mom, it hurt to see them hurt.

Now, I am not one of these moms who carry their children's successes about them as a mantle. I don't advertise their achievements to bring me glory, and I don't beat myself up for their losses, wondering what I could have done to help them more. They win and lose on their own merit. I learned a while back not to take too much credit for their good or too much blame for their bad. Yet, when they rejoice, I rejoice. And, when they hurt, I hurt.

In some ways, it seems, the umbilical cord never really gets cut. Even my boys, who I did not birth, are tied to my heartstrings forever. I think the old saying is true. The hard part about being a mom is you'll forever have pieces of your heart walking around outside your body. How difficult it can be. I've spent many a sleepless night praying for one or several of my children.

So when the Saturday of that hard week came, I decided to surprise the kids and take them all to the movies. We'd been reading *The Lion, the Witch and the Wardrobe* together, and now the movie was out. We were so excited to escape into the world of Narnia with Aslan, Peter, Susan, Edmund, and Lucy. It was an exciting movie full of adventure, danger, and the struggle between good and evil.

During one of the scary scenes, Brooke asked if she could sit on my lap. I held her tight as we watched the evil witch slay the beautiful lion. If you've read the book or seen the movie, you'll remember this scene well. The rich correlation to the crucifixion of Jesus will take your breath away. Several of my kids cried during this scene, not because of fear, but because of the truth of what Christ did for us. Through her tears, Brooke whispered in my ear, "Mommy, how does the story end? Is Aslan going to be okay? Does he win?"

I whispered back, "Brooke, you already know the answer to that question. This story is written on your heart." That's as much as I could get out before I choked up. Then my tears fell as Brooke answered back, "Yes, Mommy. I know the real story." The joy that swept over me in that moment far outweighed any accomplishment that any of my children could ever do. My children know Jesus. The real story is written on their hearts. The real story impacts their actions. The real story changes their perspectives. The real story secures their eternity.

That's a mother's greatest joy.

Think about all the questions that rumble about in a mother's heart. How are my kid's doing? Do they have good manners? Do they know what to do in an emergency? Are they being equipped to handle life outside our home? Do they handle wins and losses with grace? Are they getting a good education? Are they eating enough vegetables? Are they secure? Do they know they are loved? Are they seeing good marriage principles modeled in our home? Will they be successful in whatever job they eventually land? Will they be seen as responsible and productive? How will they handle their finances?

On and on the questions tumble about in a seemingly unending rush.

While I do want to equip my children to be well-rounded, responsible adults, I must not miss the most important thing. Of all the things I teach my children, I must place their relationship with Jesus at the top of the list. More than just going through the motions of taking them to religion classes, Sunday school, and getting them baptized, I must ask: Am I fostering in them a desire for their own personal relationship with Jesus? Yes, these other things are important outward symbols of our commitment as a family, but what about my children's hearts? Do they love Jesus out of family tradition or out of a personal relationship with Him?

Now, here's the hard part. They cannot really know Him as Healer unless He has healed them in some way. Whether it is a hurt arm, the flu, or a broken heart, do I as a mom try and take credit for making the way to healing possible? No. I take my place as the one who nurtures, but I point out that Jesus is the Healer. They cannot really know Him as Savior unless I help them understand what Jesus saves us from. I can correct, encourage, and instruct them, but I cannot save them. Only Jesus can change them, mold them, and keep their hearts pure. They cannot really know Him as Comforter if He has not comforted them in some way. Do I try and fix everything in my child's life so they never have to deal with hardship? No. I prayerfully help to a point and then step back and teach them how to turn to Jesus themselves.

Sometimes knowing how to point them to Jesus is hard. That's when I have to close my eyes and tell God the truth. "God, sometimes I have no idea what to do, and this is one of those moments." The Faithful Shepherd always answers me in the most amazing way. He teaches me how to shepherd these children and reminds me to point them to Him. The key is I have to ask. Then, I have to listen and do what He instructs. If I get no answer right away, I keep asking while I proceed ahead with this question in the forefront of my mind: What would honor God most in this situation?

In *The Lion, the Witch and the Wardrobe,* after Aslan defeats death and comes back to the children, there is a precious scene that so perfectly illustrates how personal God can be to children. "It was a romp as no one has ever had except in Narnia; and whether it was more like playing with a thunderstorm or playing with a kitten Lucy could never make up her mind. And the funny thing was that when all three finally lay together panting in the sun the girls no longer felt in the least tired or hungry or thirsty."[1]

Though my children have never rolled around play wrestling with God, they know Him and love Him. But I must continue to foster this love relationship between them and God. Life's journey is hard. The ups of life can be distracting and the downs discouraging. But all the way through, when God is front and center, they can lay down at night, panting in delight, and not feel spiritually tired or hungry for worldly recognition or thirsty for worldly wealth. They can simply be still and know that He is God and He is enough.

Yes, sweet Brooke, you know how the story ends.

Refresh My Soul

Read Psalm 78:1-7.

These verses speak of the stories of God's faithfulness being passed down from generation to generation. In biblical times there was a tradition of telling the stories of what God had done so that they would not be forgotten. This sense of God's goodness and mercy was instilled from father to son, mother to daughter throughout Israel's history. The Israelites were commanded to do this by God.

Read Deuteronomy 4:9; 6:4-9; 11:18-21.

God told the Israelites to teach their children about Him so that future generations would not be tempted to turn from Him and follow other gods. He knew that the inhabitants of the Promised Land worshipped false gods and idols and that they would influence the Israelites.

A god is anything that comes between you and your relationship with the one true God. It is anything that comes before God in your life. As you think about this definition of a god, think about the gods your children face in our culture. List some of these gods as they come to mind.

How can you, as a parent, teach your kids about Him and make Him so real and important to them that they are not tempted to follow other gods?

Read Proverbs 20:11; 1 Corinthians 13:11; 1 Peter 2:2-3.

Learning about God is a lifelong process. The process begins early on as our children first sing "Jesus Loves Me," memorize short verses, and form the habit of going to church. These first seeds of faith are planted deep within their hearts. These seeds take root as they mature. We can help with this by teaching them on their level, making God a part of their everyday lives, and allowing them to see us living out our faith.

Here are some ways we have brought God into our everyday lives:

- Playing Bible verses put to music in the car.

- Making up our own songs using Scripture verses. My daughter Ashley memorized Psalm 23 this way while we were on a long car trip.

- Reading books about missionaries' lives. Inspire your children with stories of people who lived radically for God.

- Casting a vision for who God created them to be and working to develop their unique giftings to be used for His glory.

- Talking, talking, talking about the big and little ways He is active in our lives—answering prayers, providing for our needs, and inviting us to join Him in His work on earth.

List some ways you can fill your children's hearts with the truths of God.

Read 1 Samuel 2:26; Isaiah 54:13; Luke 1:80; 2:52.

The most important part of a mom's job is to prepare our children to serve God as adults. Spend some time in prayer asking God to help you teach your children about Him. He will inspire you with creative ideas for making Him real to them if you will only ask.

"I have no greater joy than to hear that my children are walking in the truth" (3 John 4).

I pray you will know this joy as well!

6

Does God Care About Me?

*I pray that you, being rooted and established
in love, may have power, together with all
the saints, to grasp how wide and long
and high and deep is the love of Christ,
and to know this love that surpasses
knowledge—that you may be filled to
the measure of all the fullness of God.*

Ephesians 3:17-19

Does God care about you? Is He interested in the everyday details of your life? That decision you're trying to make right now, does it matter to Him?

Yes, yes, and most certainly yes.

Sometimes it is easy to wonder if God really cares about us and all the many struggles we seem to deal with on a constant basis. Here are some of the things rolling through the few brain cells I have left. How do I keep the balance between the many hats I wear? How can I be a taxi driver, mom, author, speaker, romancer of my husband, cook, maid, home organizer, exercise girl, family historian, friend, and a sane woman all at the same time? Am I the woman God wants me to be? Am I pleasing Him?

I can only please God and fulfill my many roles by living a life of complete dependence on Him. By bringing these verses to my mind often, I find wonderful peace: "The Lord is near. Do not be anxious about anything, but in everything, by prayer and petition, with thanksgiving, present your requests to God. And the peace of God, which transcends all understanding, will guard your hearts and your minds in Christ Jesus" (Philippians 4:5-7).

Where this peace starts to slip is when I try and figure God out. I try to reason my way into the peace rather than praying and making the choice to stop all my toil and wondering and leave them in God's hands. Accept each step God puts before me as my temporary assignment, fulfill that part of it, and leave the rest with Him.

Just yesterday God showed me this truth lived out in such a powerful way. We had a little bird fly into one of the windows in our house. He fell to the ground below, unable to move and barely able to chirp. Our two youngest daughters, Brooke and Ashley, saw what happened and were so upset for the precious little bird. They came bounding into my bedroom right in the middle of a much-needed and much-desired nap.

Though I felt as much compassion as my sleepy heart could muster up, I did not want to get out of bed. So I whispered to them that they could give the bird some cracker crumbs, drops of water, and pray over him until Mommy finished her nap. Now, I fully intended to get up shortly thereafter and go "help God" help the birdie fly away so my daughters' prayers could be answered. Isn't it funny how we moms sometimes think we have to help God? It's as if we say, "God, I do trust You, but just in case You are too busy today, I'm going to fill in Your gaps." Or, out of a sincere desire for what we think is best for our child, we say, "God, I really know this child and have a keen insight into this situation, so bless my efforts as I step in and fix a few things." We say we trust God with our kids, but do we really?

The girls went outside, put gloves on, and stroked the bird while telling it that everything would be all right. They also put out cracker crumbs and water and then prayed over the bird. Little Brooke's prayers must have taken longer than what Ashley had patience for because Brooke was left alone with the bird for an extended period of time.

Brooke loves to pray, so her prayers were very bold over this hurting bird. About an hour later she came to wake me from my nap and ask me to check on the bird. I was so afraid we'd find our feathered friend dead. I hadn't gotten up in time to help God out! Oh dear, what will become of my sweet girl's faith in prayer? But Brooke walked confidently toward the bird that was still lying beneath the window. As we were almost close enough to touch him, he suddenly sat up, chirped at us, and flew off. Brooke jumped up and down and clapped her little hands while exclaiming, "God heard my prayers and He answered my prayers!"

I was brought to tears as I leaned down and told her, "For the rest of your life remember how real God is and how He always hears your prayers."

As these words of truth came out of my mouth, God nudged my heart as if to say, "I want you to remember the same thing you just told your daughter." Sweet friend, His eye is on the sparrow and, even more so, on you and your precious children.

For the rest of that day, we were delightfully serenaded by this sweet bird as he danced from window to window outside our home. I pray God lets you hear the songs of the birds today and for many tomorrows to come so that you can know He sees you, He hears you, He cares about you, and He most certainly loves you!

Refresh My Soul

Read Psalm 84:1-4.

God cares enough about all of His creation to find a home even for the smallest, most insignificant of creatures.

Now read Matthew 10:29-31. What do verses 30 and 31 tell you about how God feels about you? Write down your feelings after reading this.

Did you know that you are that important to God?

"Even the very hairs on your head are numbered" (Matthew 10:30). Read 1 Samuel 14:45; 2 Samuel 14:11; Luke 21:18; Acts 27:34.

God is so aware of our lives that not even a hair on our heads will fall to the ground without His knowledge. After I had my babies, my hair would fall out in clumps. According to these verses, God was aware of every hair that fell. How amazing!

"You are worth more than many sparrows" (Matthew 10:31). Read Matthew 6:26; 12:11-12.

God gave us dominion over His creation. Genesis 1:28 says, "God blessed [Adam and Eve] and said to them, 'Be fruitful and increase in number; fill the earth and subdue it. Rule over the fish of the sea and the birds of the air and over every living creature that moves on the ground.'" We are so much more valuable to Him than the animals and birds. We have eternal souls He invites to spend with Him.

The truth is, God loved us so much that He sent Jesus to save us. Don't let how often you have heard that statement diminish the impact of it. Many of us have memorized John 3:16, but have we really taken time to meditate on the truth that verse contains? "For God so loved the world that he gave his one and only Son, that whoever believes in him shall not perish but have eternal life."

For God so loved the world.

For God so loved you.

Read Romans 5:8; Ephesians 2:4-5; 1 John 4:9-10.

There are numerous verses about God's love for us. It is too much for our human minds to comprehend, really. I will leave you with some verses to think about as you try to wrap your mind around God's love for you:

> I pray that you, being rooted and established in love, may have power, together with all the saints, to grasp how wide and long and high and deep is the love of Christ, and to know this love that surpasses knowledge—that you may be filled to the measure of all the fullness of God (Ephesians 3:17-19).

This is my prayer for you, and I hope that you will make it your prayer for yourself.

7

Did I Really Just Say That?

The heart itself is only a small vessel,
yet dragons are there, and lions,
there are poisonous beasts,
and all the treasures of evil,
there are rough and uneven roads,
there are precipes;
but there too is God and the angels,
life is there, and the Kingdom,
there too is light, and there the apostles
and heavenly cities,
and treasures of grace.
All things lie within that little space.

MAKARIOS THE GREAT

It had been a great day. The house was tidy. The dinner was Crock-Potting away, filling the house with delicious smells. The kids had completed their schoolwork and were now happily playing outside. My husband called from out of town to let me know he was having a great time, and I bragged about how well everyone was doing here on the home front. Now I had a few minutes to steal away and read. I picked up my book, settled on the couch, and smiled.

Three sentences into the first page, my great day started going south. The happy little people playing in the yard came thundering into the house, having turned into grumpy, hot, messy creatures intent on wreaking havoc in my sanctuary. "Mom, my straw busted through the bottom of my drink," one cried as she carried the dripping cup through the living room, through the kitchen, and parked in front of me on the den carpet. I jumped from the couch, grabbed the drink, and turned to find another creature standing behind me, her new church outfit covered in mud. Then started the whining in the kitchen from one staring down at the Crock-Pot. "Why can't we be like normal families and eat out at restaurants? We always eat at home."

With all my might I wanted to give a June Cleaver sweet answer that included the words "That's all right, dear, and it would be swell to eat out sometime." But I couldn't find her inside me. I gritted my teeth and said, "Sweetheart," (don't you love how this word takes on a completely different meaning when spoken through gritted teeth?) "did it ever cross your mind to leave the dripping cup outside instead of carrying the sticky, orange, carpet-staining juice throughout the house?"

I then turned to mud girl. "Why are we wearing our nice clothes to play outside?" I shook my head in disbelief while thinking, *We have drawers full of play clothes that have seen better days. But to play in the mud, of course only church clothes will do.*

And to the Crock-Pot complainer who couldn't have picked a worse time, I wanted to go into a long diatribe about what it took to go to the store, buy the food, bring it home, unload it, and prepare it. But I was up to my elbows in mud and orange juice, so I fired off a quick answer about the expense of going out to eat and how he should be more grateful. I gave up on the book reading and with a frustrated huff finished cleaning and called everyone to an early dinner.

That didn't go as I would have liked either, and by the end of the meal I'd had enough. I stood up at the end of the table, cleared my throat in a very dramatic fashion, and announced it was time for everyone to go to bed. "But it's still light outside," they protested. I had no idea what time the clock said, and frankly I didn't care. Bedtime was going to rescue me, and I was a woman on a mission. To add even more drama to my announcement, I concluded by saying that after they got ready for bed they should go sit on their beds and moan...for the Bible says that the Holy Spirit will lift up prayers on our behalf if all we can do is moan. "So the Holy Spirit will be tucking you into bed tonight. I am done!"

I turned, grabbed the book I never got to read, and marched off to my bedroom. Mommy was putting herself in a time-out!

I plopped down on my bed and stared at the ceiling. Did I just tell my kids that the Holy Spirit would be tucking them into bed? What kind of mother does that? *A tired, exhausted, empty one,* I answered myself. One who had not turned her emotions over to the Lord today. One who had not taken time before rushing into her day to ask the Lord to be her portion and to give her His perspective throughout the day. One who hadn't taken time to pray.

I pushed the book I'd been waiting to read all afternoon aside and reached for my Bible.

> Because of the LORD's great love we are not consumed, for his compassions never fail. They are new every morning; great is your faithfulness. I say to myself, "The LORD is my *portion;* therefore I will wait for him" (Lamentations 3:22-24, emphasis added).

> My flesh and my heart may fail, but God is the strength of my heart and my *portion* forever (Psalm 73:26, emphasis added).

Even Jesus, the Savior of the world, had to take time each day to ask for His portion. When He taught us to pray in Matthew 6, He taught us to ask for our portion. Matthew 6:11 says, "Give us today our daily bread."

Do you remember when the children of Israel were wandering in the desert waiting to be delivered to the Promise Land? God rained down manna, small flakes of food from heaven, just enough for each day. He didn't allow them to gather storehouses full of manna because *He* wanted to be their daily portion. He wanted them to come to Him each day and recognize their need for Him. He delighted in them asking, and He delighted in providing for them every time they asked. That's how they grew from seeing God as a religious being to having a real relationship with Him.

That's how we grow as well. The reality is that we will all have days where our attitude is not what it should be. We all fall short. Now, maybe you've never fallen as short as me, the woman who relied on the Holy Spirit to tuck her kids into bed! But there are areas in which you will have to rely on God and His provision.

As moms it is so easy to let our emotions run wild and operate based on how we feel. If we feel happy, we can be patient. But if our stress level rises, it is easy to let our patience slip and snap at those we love most. If we feel organized, we can be stable. But if things start getting misplaced and disheveled, it is easy to feel angry and fly off the handle. This roller coaster of emotions is hard on mom and family.

I've found the only stabilizing force when I feel my emotions running away is the Lord. Praying these "portion" Scriptures and asking God to be my portion is a daily discipline. I can't just will myself to be in a good mood and act godly; I have to rely on God's strength, power, control, and provision.

Spend some time today asking yourself if you are in control of your emotions or letting your emotions control you. Whatever your shortcoming, God is waiting for you to ask for His portion every day and He will provide. When we allow Him to reign in us, His portion will rain on us.

Refresh My Soul

Read Psalm 4.

This is a psalm of hope. David writes of God's protection, peace, and provision. He knows that God will keep him safe and grant him what he needs. His trust is in God.

I especially like verse 4, when David talks about sitting on our beds and being silent. How I wish I could have read that verse before I said what I said! My kids have for sure heard me say some things when I should have kept silent, as this verse recommends. Are there times in your life when you wish you had stayed silent? Are there things you regret saying to your kids or your husband?

Our words are powerful. Indeed, the tongue is the strongest muscle in the body. How we use that muscle makes all the difference. James 3:5 says, "The tongue is a small part of the body, but it makes great boasts. Consider what a great forest is set on fire by a small spark."

Read Psalm 34:13; 39:1; Proverbs 10:19; 21:23.

How can we, as moms, watch our words and train our tongues?

Our words can be used to build up or tear down. We can speak words of encouragement or we can speak words of destruction. We can think before we speak or we can react without thinking about the effect of our words. These are choices we make every time we open our mouths. Sitting on my bed and being silent is sounding better and better!

Here are some good and bad ways we use our words:

- Praising—Psalm 71:24

- Praying—Psalm 86:6

- Singing—Psalm 119:172

- Lying—Proverbs 6:16-19

- Flattering—Proverbs 28:23

- Teaching—Proverbs 31:26

- Worshipping—Philippians 2:11

- Arguing—2 Timothy 2:23

"Sticks and stones can break my bones, but words will never hurt me," the old saying goes. That could not be further from the truth. Words do hurt. Our words have so much power. Proverbs 25:15 says, "Through patience a ruler can be persuaded, and a gentle tongue can break a bone."

Have you given much thought to the power of your words? Spend some time writing about times when you have chosen your words carefully and times when you have not. Examine the effects of your choices.

"A man finds joy in giving an apt reply—and how good is a timely word!" (Proverbs 15:23).

"A word aptly spoken is like apples of gold in settings of silver" (Proverbs 25:11).

We must choose our words carefully. We can't just say whatever we think and blurt things out haphazardly. What we say with our tongues reaches far beyond the moment. The words we use will often stay with someone forever. We cannot take back our words once we say them. All we can do is pray for God to fill in our gaps, forgive us when we mess up, and be our portion each day so that we do not reach the end of ourselves.

8

This Crazy Little Thing
Called Love

*Love does not consist in gazing at
each other, but in looking outward
together in the same direction.*

ANTOINE DE SAINT-EXUPERY

Cleaning my office last week, I came across an envelope with hearts all over the outside and a gift certificate inside. I was so thrilled to have found this unexpected surprise! I eagerly opened it and discovered that it was a gift certificate to Victoria Secret. *Oh, her,* I thought, a little disappointed. Not that I don't like sweet Victoria. It's just that she is a reminder that my post-kid body leaves a lot to be desired. The thought of wearing something that is scratchy, over-revealing, and undersized just doesn't give me the motivation I need to make a special trip to the mall.

I guess when I got it, I just filed it away with good intentions to use it when my taste buds die, my body shrinks, and muscles suddenly appear in all the right places. When had I received this little treasure? Upon closer investigation, I doubled over in laughter as I realized the certificate was more than ten years old! Art came over to see what was so funny, so I handed him the certificate. He found no humor in the situation and offered to take it off my hands and use it to buy me a gift. I just smiled back at him and requested that he remember two things on his shopping trip: warmth and comfort. Does Victoria make flannel pj's?

Whether it is because of changes in our bodies, sleep deprivation, time constraints, financial pressures, or a myriad of other things, marriage changes after kids. But it doesn't have to be for the worse. We must still make our marriage a priority and watch it grow stronger through the kid years. After all, one of the greatest gifts parents can give their children is the security of a solid love relationship between Mom and Dad.

Realizing this greatest gift, I wanted to see what the Bible says the love in a marriage is supposed to look like by using 1 Corinthians 13:4-8 as a guide. This passage of Scripture clearly lays out God's design for love and the legacy that can be built when these characteristics define a marriage:

> Love is patient, love is kind. It does not envy, it does not boast, it is not proud. It is not rude, it is not self-seeking, it is not easily angered, it keeps no record of wrongs. Love does not delight in evil but rejoices with the truth. It always protects, always trusts, always hopes, always perseveres. Love never fails.

As I read these verses, I am always challenged. If I'm really honest with myself, this does not always describe the love I have for my husband. What I'm reminded of is that this type of love does not just happen when you say "I do." This is not a passive, descriptive kind of love you inherit on your wedding day. This is an active love. This is me deciding to make my love characterized by these qualities and choosing to do whatever I can to make it true for my relationship.

Art and I decided to take an honest assessment of our marriage using this definition of love. Then we had an honest talk about what our strengths and weaknesses are. After identifying places that needed to be worked on, we wrote out Scripture verses to pray for each other's weak spots. Here is what we wrote:

1 Corinthians 13:4-8 Assessment

Am I patient with my spouse? (I am flexible and understanding.)
EPHESIANS 4:2-3

Am I kind to my spouse? (I am kind in thought, words, and actions toward them.) EPHESIANS 4:31-32

Am I supportive (not envious) with my spouse? (I do not keep score when I feel I do more.) JAMES 3:16-18

Am I encouraging (not boastful) to my spouse? (I do not brag about my accomplishments while downplaying theirs.)
HEBREWS 3:13

Am I humble (not proud) with my spouse? (I do not think my agenda is more important than my spouse's agenda.)
1 PETER 5:6

Am I gracious (not rude) to my spouse? (I build up my spouse with my words spoken in private and public.) EPHESIANS 4:29

Am I selfless (not self-seeking) with my spouse? (I focus on my spouse's needs and wants and balance them with my own.)
PHILIPPIANS 2:3-4

Am I self-controlled (not easily angered) with my spouse? (I do not have a short fuse or quick temper.) PROVERBS 15:1

Am I able to forgive and let go (keeping no record of wrongs) with my spouse's shortcomings? (I do not use my spouse's past shortcomings as ammunition in today's disagreements or allow these things to taint our communication today.)
COLOSSIANS 3:12-14

Do I delight in being faithful to God (not delighting in evil)? (I seek to live a pure life and choose not to flirt with sin.)
EPHESIANS 4:1

Do I rejoice with the truth? (I actively pursue God's truth over Satan's lies.) JOHN 8:31-32

Do I seek to protect my spouse? (I fill in the gaps where they feel weak and vulnerable.) 1 THESSALONIANS 5:11

Do I trust my spouse? (I give my spouse the benefit of the doubt.) 1 PETER 3:8

Do I keep hope alive in my marriage? (I trust God with "our" future, not "my" future.) JEREMIAH 29:11

Do I persevere in my marriage? (I look for solutions to problems rather than look for a way out.) MATTHEW 5:33

Am I committed to the permanence of our marriage? (I believe that divorce is not an option for us.) MALACHI 2:16

In the scramble of handling all the details of a life full of little people, romance and love can sometimes take a backseat. We have to not only be intentional with our active love, but also be intentional about keeping our love fresh, exciting, and fun. You can't compare your circumstances and relationship with others; that will only serve to drain and discourage you. Keep your focus on making your marriage the best it can be. It is what you put into your marriage that you'll be able to pull out of your marriage. The grass isn't greener on the other side; it is greener where you water and fertilize it.

Water and fertilize the love in your marriage by making priority investments:

- Take the 1 Corinthians 13:4-8 assessment.
- Go out on regularly scheduled date nights.
- Share prayer requests with each other.
- Pray for your family together.
- Set some goals for your relationship.
- Make a habit to write each other love notes.

- Attend a marriage conference or read a marriage book together.

- Decide on a dream vacation for the two of you and start saving money to make it happen.

- Become a student of your spouse and keep a journal of what you learn about them.

- Add to this list specific things that are special in your relationship.

Maybe my little hidden gift certificate was a sign that I need to make some adjustments and investments. I think I'll ask Art if I can accompany him to the mall. And no, I won't be in search of flannel.

Refresh My Soul

Read Psalm 37:23-24.

Make no mistake, Satan does not want your marriage to succeed. He wants you to fail. He wants your marriage to be another statistic. He wants to keep you from treating each other with kindness and love. He wants to get between you any way he can. Why? Because he knows that if he can break up families, he will hinder the kingdom of God. The family was God's building block for all of earth. He began with one man and one woman. He placed them together to accomplish His purposes.

All marriages are bound to face trouble at some point. Chances are, your marriage has already faced trouble, is facing trouble, or will face trouble in the future. You may have read this chapter with deep sadness in your heart. You might be thinking, *My marriage is too far gone for that.* Please don't give up! Turn to the God of hope with the future of your marriage (Romans 15:13).

Remember that you are not fighting the battle for your marriage alone. God wants you to succeed. He wants to give you the victory. You need only to join Him. Here are some verses to inspire you:

> The LORD will fight for you; you need only to be still (Exodus 14:14).

> All those gathered here will know that it is not by sword or spear that the LORD saves; for the battle is the LORD's (1 Samuel 17:47).

> Be strong and courageous. Do not be afraid or discouraged because of the king of Assyria and the vast army with him, for there is a greater power with us than with him. With him is only the arm of flesh, but with us is the LORD our God to help us and to fight our battles (2 Chronicles 32:7-8).

There will be times that you feel like giving up. You will not want to work on your marriage and will despair of ever reaching a place of confidence. When that happens, let these verses encourage you to work at your marriage and to stand firm in your convictions:

> My dear [sisters], stand firm. Let nothing move you. Always give yourselves fully to the work of the Lord, because you know that your labor in the Lord is not in vain (1 Corinthians 15:58).

> Whatever you do, work at it with all your heart, as working for the Lord, not for men (Colossians 3:23).

God loves you. He loves your husband. He brought the two of you together for such a time as this. You can choose to press forward with God's help or give up and give Satan the victory.

My prayer is that you will choose to stand—and someday have an amazing testimony of God's faithfulness. He can work a miracle in your marriage.

In the meantime, I want to challenge you to pray for your marriage. Pray that you would be able to see your husband as God sees him. Pray that he will be able to do the same for you. Pray that you both will be able to see beyond yourselves. Pray that you will be able to humbly submit to God's will for your marriage. Write down a prayer for your marriage today. Use any Scriptures God lays on your heart. Commit to pray daily for your marriage, and wait expectantly for God's blessings when you do!

9

The Great Lover
of My Soul

Love doesn't make the world go 'round.
Love is what makes the ride worthwhile.

FRANKLIN P. JONES

Don't you just adore a good love story? You know, the kind that makes your heart beat fast as you're not quite sure whether the guy will eventually get the girl. There is an obvious attraction, tension in chase, some life circumstance that seeks to pull them apart, and then the story culminates in the final scene with a kiss that seals the deal for a lifetime. Why are we so moved by these love stories? I believe it is because God designed our hearts for an eternal love story, our love story with Jesus.

But many of the women I talk with are so caught up in the busyness of raising kids that they have lost sight of their first love. Instead of serving God out of delight, they slip into serving Him out of duty. One woman said, "I love God, but I'm sad to say my actions don't reflect that very often. I always seem to be answering the urgent calls of my children. Therefore, I never quite make time to hear God's voice." Another woman came up to me at a conference in tears and said, "When I was in college, I studied my Bible and made time for God. Now I feel so distant from Him. I've stopped trying to spend time with Him because putting a quiet time on my to-do list made me feel like a failure when I never got to it."

When we serve God merely out of duty, we add religious items to our already full days: read the Bible, spend time in prayer, go to church, serve in some ministry, and keep a good Christian smile on while doing it all. God's life-giving principles are reduced to another set of rules we're forced to follow. Instead of refilling and refreshing us, our relationship with God becomes another source of stress. Why does this happen and how do we change this? How do we capture the love our souls were designed for and let it change us for good?

Praise God for the Good

We start by recognizing that all that is good in our lives comes from God and praising Him for that. It is so easy to get distracted by what is wrong in our lives and take for granted all that is good. Let's list all that is good about different areas of our life. Fill in your list below:

Things that are good about my relationship with the Lord:

1. I know Jesus is my Savior.

2.

3.

4.

5.

Things that are good about my marriage:

1.

2.

3.

4.

5.

Things that are good about me as a mother:

1.

2.

3.

4.

5.

Things that are good about my kids:

1.

2.

3.

4.

5.

Things that are good about my home:

1.

2.

3.

   4.

   5.

Things that are good about my friends:

   1.

   2.

   3.

   4.

   5.

Things that are good about my finances:

   1.

   2.

   3.

   4.

   5.

Things that are good about my ministry:

   1.

   2.

   3.

   4.

   5.

Now spend some time praising God for each of these things. If you had a hard time with any of the categories, ask Him to reveal things you can be thankful for, even if they are really small things. For the next week, make it a habit to look at your list often. Maybe you'll even want to continue to add to it. The main point is to use this list as a starting place to begin an attitude of praise for your first love.

A Tug Toward Eternity

We must also recognize the longings in our heart as a tug toward eternity, not a sign that our lives here are less than blessed. I love the Serenity Prayer, which speaks of having the courage to change the things I can, accepting the things I cannot change, and having the wisdom to know the difference. This wisdom "to know the difference" is where the tug for eternity comes into play. When a longing in my heart starts discouraging me, I make the choice to turn it around by seeing it as a reminder of my first love. If nothing here ever disappointed me, I would be tempted to become satisfied without Jesus.

Instead of letting my disappointments discourage me, I let my heart be drawn toward Jesus and ask Him to fill me. If I have an argument with my husband, Jesus fill me. If I'm discouraged by the actions of my children, Jesus fill me. If I am hurt by another, Jesus fill me. When my favorite trinket gets broken, Jesus fill me. When I outgrow my favorite jeans, Jesus fill me. When I spill bleach on my favorite shirt, Jesus fill me. When my car door gets dinged by an uncaring person in the car next to me, Jesus fill me. When the store clerk is rude, Jesus fill me. When the dog chews up my new rug, Jesus fill me. When all my pictures in the digital camera get erased, Jesus fill me. When I'm emotionally overwhelmed, Jesus fill me.

Tug my heart, point my eyes, and lift up my soul toward eternity, Lord. Help me to see all these disappointments as temporary and not worth getting all worked up over. When I feel myself getting empty over worldly things, fill me, Jesus. Help me return to my first love.

This is easy to say but hard to do in the heat of the moment. But take heart! The Holy Spirit is our Steady Comforter and our Ready Reminder. We don't have to do this in our own strength. We simply let Jesus' name fall from our lips, and the Holy Spirit will give us the comfort we need and remind us how to react.

It All Hinges on a Choice

When it comes right down to it, everything hinges on one simple yet complex six-letter word. If you had to guess what this word might be, what would you say? Wealth? Health? Esteem? Dreams? Chance? No, I would have to say the word "choice." Knowing how to make good choices determines a lot in life. When to go, when to stay...when to stop, when to start...when to push, when to pull back...when to rush, when to slow down...when to say yes, when to say no...when to believe, when to doubt...when to spend, when to save...when to fly high, when to stay low...these choices are a gift and a curse all wrapped up in one. When God gave us the ability to choose, He gave us a beautiful thing. Free will makes our choice to love Him true, genuine, and eternally significant.

At the same time, what a tragedy that God gave us the ability to choose. For mankind's wrong choice to sin caused a separation from God that only the death of His Son, Jesus, could repair. But I trust our all-knowing and all-powerful God, and I take His gift of choice with a prayerful and sometimes trembling heart.

I know my own propensity toward bad choices. I have made my fair share of them. The sad part is, I usually know when I'm making a bad choice, yet my self-centered flesh forges ahead past all the warning signals flashing through my mind. I do fine with the rules-of-life choices. I am a rule-follower by nature. I don't reuse postage stamps missed by the cancellation mark, I return my grocery cart to a designated place, and if I ever found a bundle of cash, I would seek to give it back to its rightful owner.

No, the choice I struggle with is letting the Spirit of Christ, my first love, have full reign in me. I want to model a gentle, quiet spirit, but what a struggle it is for this wild-blooded Italian woman! So much of my life hinges on this one choice. I have to consciously return to my first love every day. In big ways and small, I have to make the choice to reveal the reality of Jesus in my life. Praising Him, feeling those tugs toward eternity, and consciously choosing my first love will do more to fill me than anything else.

Refresh My Soul

Read Psalm 63:1; 119:20; 119:174.

"He has made everything beautiful in its time. He has also set eternity in the hearts of men; yet they cannot fathom what God has done from beginning to end" (Ecclesiastes 3:11).

Read Genesis 21:33.

This verse refers to God as "El Olam" or "the God of Eternity." Our souls are crying out for God. We have an indwelling sense of there being more to life than just the things of this earth. Deep down, we know that eternity is part of our makeup. God has placed within us a deep need for Him. I have heard it said that we all have a "God-shaped hole" in our hearts that nothing else can fill. Many people try to fill that hole with flimsy substitutes. Alcohol and other addictions, the love of people, money, and other things serve as substitutes that just can't give us what we long for. Many people sadly spend their whole lives searching for something to fill what their soul is longing for.

Is there something you are trying to fill that hole with right now? Don't listen to Satan's lies that a substitute will work. Pray for God to show you how to fill that hole with Him and Him only.

Read Psalm 71:5-8.

Our souls were created to love God, our bodies were created to serve God, and our mouths were created to praise God. From the depths of our hearts, we should pour forth praise and thanks for all that He has done for us. Our basic attitude as we go through our days should be an attitude of praise.

Is this your attitude?

An attitude of praise does not require one more check mark on your growing to-do list. It does not require stress or obligation. It requires a heart that is sold out for God, a heart that loves Him not for what He does, but for who He is. Don't make your love and gratitude conditional. When things are going wrong, praise Him anyway! Thank Him in advance for the good He will surely bring from all situations (Romans 8:28).

This is easier said than done, you say? Try it! Just for one day, determine to honor Him with your praises. Play praise music in your home. Sing to Him. Sure, your kids may think you've lost your mind, but do it anyway! Be intentional about your attitude of praise. Don't let Satan steal your outlook and your perspective.

The psalms are filled with praise. David did not only praise God when things were going right in his life; he praised Him when he was running for his life, when he lost a child, when he felt far away from God, and when his dreams did not come true. David was called a man after God's own heart (1 Samuel 13:14). I think his basic attitude of praise was a large part of that. Using the psalms to inspire you, write your own psalm of praise.

A Refueled Approach

10

I Love Smelly Shoes

Be thankful. Cultivate an "attitude of gratitude." Thankfulness is much more dependent on attitude than circumstance. When you feel the lack of what you don't have, thank God for what you do have! At any time, there is more going right in the life of a committed Christian than there is going wrong. It's just that the "wrong" makes a lot more noise than the "right."

JIM STEPHENS

The art of thanksgiving is one that we should all pass on to our children. I'm not talking about the holiday with pumpkin pie and turkey. I'm not talking about decorating with cornucopias, dried corn stalks, and scarecrows. I'm not talking about setting a candlelit table with fancy linens and fine silver. While those are all artistic ways of expressing the day of Thanksgiving, I'm talking about the attitude of thankfulness that can so easily become overlooked. I'm talking about the art of saying "thank you."

I am so blessed. But I'm also guilty of becoming so distracted by my blessings that I forget to thank the One from whose hands these things come. Do I see the loving husband I've been blessed with, or do I just grumble about his faults? Do I see the creative child I am blessed with, or do I just grumble about her artistic messes? Do I see the health of a son who can play sports as a blessing, or do I just grumble about his sweaty laundry? Do I see the home I am blessed with, or do I just grumble about the constant chores to keep it clean? Do I see how blessed we are to have food whenever we want, or do I just grumble about a kitchen that never seems to stay clean? You get the picture.

I decided I wanted to be more intentional with expressing my thankfulness. I also wanted to be more intentional with developing an attitude of thankfulness in my children. I want the words "thank you" to fall so easily from their lips that it becomes second nature. Without thinking or much effort, they say "thank you" for both the big and small. I want them to say it to the Lord, people they know, and even those they don't know but should express gratitude to.

Realizing I must model what I teach, I decided to assess how thankful I really am. As I made a mental list for those things I was thankful for, I suddenly became distracted with an unusual amount of out-of-place shoes scattered about my home. Not so spiritual, I know. But the shoes seemed to be coming out of the woodwork and screaming for my attention. I went from being a blessed woman with a full heart focused on God to a grumbling woman suddenly feeling frustrated and drained. How many times have I picked up shoes? In my motherhood journey, how many shoes will I pick up and put back, only to pick them up and put them back again...and again...and again?

I counted 14 pairs of shoes that were just within eyesight of where I was sitting. Upon further inspection, they were every-where—by the back door, the front door, in the laundry room, in the hallway, in the kitchen, by the dog dish, on the stairs, in the guest bathroom, in my bathroom, on the floor in the kids' bedrooms, and even in the linen closet. I was quite frustrated that these shoes weren't where they were supposed to be. Visions of chore charts and consequences for leaving things out and about started dancing in my mind. I even went so far as to think that this was yet more evidence that my kids are not as thankful as they should be. Kids who were truly thankful for their shoes would care enough to tuck them into their closet shoe racks.

But as I mentally chided my children for their ungratefulness, I felt God gently give me a piece of my own reprimand. Was I modeling what I wanted my kids to model in their lives? Scattered shoes are a normal, everyday thing with a hidden treasure about them. How I chose to look at those shoes would determine whether I felt drained and frustrated or filled up and thankful.

I stopped and thanked God for this evidence of life. Some had grass and dirt on them as proof that our kids are healthy and strong enough to run and play. Some had scuff marks from one too many dances on the concrete outside. Some had teeth marks from our beloved dog, Champ, who's favorite pastime is chasing kids, balls, and stray shoes. One had paint on it from a school project. All were well worn, broken in, and definitely used.

So here I am, on life's journey in a season of soccer cleats, princess shoes, basketball high-tops, teenager wannabe boots, kitten bedroom slippers, and gymnastics flip-flops. Funny how these shoes tell stories of life, if only I make the choice to listen. Games won and lost, girlhood fantasies, dreams of the future, comforts of home, and expressions of style.

Maybe you've felt a little frustrated with the shoes scattered about your home. But the next time you pick them up, instead of letting frustration whisk you away, listen carefully to the story they tell. Listen carefully and thank God for each and every evidence of life.

I put the shoes in a big pile in the middle of my kitchen and took a picture. They weren't neatly arranged and perfectly matched. They were just scattered and tossed about. It looked like a little shoe party, and all sizes and shapes had been invited. I think I'll frame this picture and let it remind me often of the beauty of a refueled approach.

How I look at things makes a world of difference. If my approach is one that living life simply drains me, then I'll constantly feel drained. But if I can pull back the veil and peek behind the messes, chores, and faults of others, I'll see the treasure of what these things represent. I'm a wife! I'm a mom! I have the privilege to fulfill these eternally significant roles for some pretty amazing people...my family!

What about my thankful list? I eventually got back to that. I'm thankful for the gift of our Savior. I am thankful for my husband and kids. I am thankful for friends and extended family. I am thankful for our home full of life and lots of activity. And strangely enough, I'm really thankful for shoes...especially the smelly ones!

Refresh My Soul

Read Psalm 56:13; 66:8-9; Proverbs 4:25-27; Luke 1:79; Hebrews 12:13.

Have you ever stopped to think about the smelly shoes in your house? How about all those stinky socks? (Perhaps in heaven we will learn where all the missing socks in our homes disappeared to!) You might not see smelly shoes and stinky socks as the blessings of motherhood, but today we are going to look at what God has to say about the feet that go in those shoes and socks. They are the feet of those you love best in the world.

We use our feet to get us where we need to go. They take us wherever we point them—whether good or bad, right or wrong. As you think of the shoes in your house, think of where those feet are taking those you love. Are they making good choices? Are they honoring God with their words and actions wherever they go?

The verses you read today assure us that God watches over our feet. Psalm 40:2 says, "He set my feet upon a rock and gave me a firm place to stand." He cares about where our feet take us, and He wants even our feet to honor Him. Have you ever heard the expression, "My feet came out from under me"? He does not want us to slip or fall. How does He accomplish this? By making our paths straight and giving us a light to guide our way. Psalm 119:105 says, "Your word is a lamp to my feet and a light for my path."

These words assure us that God can and will provide a way for us to honor Him with our feet. We can stay on the path that leads to righteousness by staying in the Word, by fixing our eyes on Him, and praying for His direction.

I want to urge you to do something that might feel silly. Pray over your children's shoes. The next time you trip over a stray tennis shoe, pray for the little foot that belongs in it. The next time you notice a wayward flip-flop outside, pray for the little pink-painted toes that left it behind. The next time you find a large pair of men's loafers kicked off by the door, pray for the large responsibility that rests on those feet. The next time you fold laundry and find socks that are missing their mates, thank God for blessing you with loved ones to fold laundry for. And if you find an actual matched pair, it's time to praise Him!

11

Super Mom vs. Slacker Mom

A halo has to fall only a few inches to become a noose.

FARMER'S ALMANAC

Which hat should I wear today? Let's look at the many options. Here's a beautiful Southern Belle brimmed hat…my fashionable friends would love that. Oh, and a baseball cap…my husband would think that looks very cute on me. Then there's the white nurse hat trimmed in red ribbon…let's hope no one needs me to wear this today. Yikes, here's a black pointy one…let's put that one in the trash. And of course all my mom hats: the chauffeur, the handyman, the project helper, the editor, the teacher, the cook, the maid, the activities coordinator, the vacation planner, and the family historian. But a hat should fully express who I am, not just what role I am playing at the time. And to be honest, I don't like hats that much. I think I'll tie my hair up in a clip and just be me today.

That's a hard thing for us moms anymore...to just be ourselves. We are caught up in this strange era of defining ourselves by what kind of mom other people see us as. I spent my day today doing research about the titles defining mothers and found some interesting debates. Basically, there seems to be a continuum where mothers at one end are sporting a professionally designed graphics art masterpiece that reads "Super Moms Are the Best and, By the Way, My Kid Beat Your Kid in the Spelling Bee...Again!" At the other end there's a ragtag-looking hand-scribbled poster that reads "Slacker Moms Rule...and the Thought of Spending Hours Memorizing Spelling Words Makes Us Nauseous."

I found books, movies, television shows, magazine articles, and blogs galore written about this debate. Interestingly, when I did a search on "overparenting," there were 663 results. But when I did a search for "slacker mom" there was a whopping 22,000 results. Hmm...it seems that slacker moms have more time to spend on the computer. Hey, I spent quite a bit of time on the computer today—maybe I'm a slacker mom? But then just yesterday I spent 12 hours taking my daughter to her gymnastics meet. I drove her there, watched her compete, praised her for a job well done, and took her out to dinner afterward. Maybe I'm overparenting? Or maybe I'm just doing the best I can and don't really fit in either camp.

Just as I don't like hats, I don't like labels, either. I want to be a good mom for the kids God has entrusted to my care. I don't want to be a slacker mom or a supermom. I just want to be the kind of mom God intends for me to be. I want to be a unique mom with gifts, talents, attitudes, beliefs, and convictions all my own. Because I surrender my heart and my walk to God every day, I believe He gives me wisdom to handle just what I need to handle each and every day. I want to be me, and I'm okay with that. Some days I'll be a little more like a slacker. Other days I might feel a little supermomish. But most days I'm just going to do the best I can with the circumstances I'm handed.

Maybe you're wondering what each end of this parenting spectrum looks like. The supermom who overparents is the mom who is always at every one of her child's activities. She calls the teacher about each grade lower than an A. Some refer to her as the helicopter mom who hovers over her child's every move. She's the room mom, the soccer mom, and the volunteer extraordinaire. She has good intentions, but she must stop and ask herself why she's doing all this. I suspect she wants her child to excel, but lurking behind this involvement is the reality that she wants to make herself look good as well. She wants people to look at her child and give her accolades. "Wow, that child is really doing well in school. She must have a great mom." "Wow, that child scored the most goals at the game. She must have a great mom." "Wow, that child is so well behaved. She must have a great mom." "Wow, that child had the most extravagant science fair project. She must have a great mom."

Is having a smart, successful kid a bad thing? Of course not, but when we do what we do for the recognition it brings us, we become out of balance. A dangerous message is sent to kids when a parent is overly involved. It tells the child that the parent loves them for what they do, not simply for who they are. It also tells the child that the parent does not trust them to be able to succeed on their own. "Little Johnny, Mommy is going to help make sure your project is the best. Oh, sweetie, don't glue that there. Let's glue these here. Actually, just let Mommy do it." In other words, Johnny, you can't do it right—you don't measure up. How proud is little Johnny really going to be when he gets a grade he knows his mom deserves, not him?

Ouch…these are stinging words. Because, honestly, what mom hasn't helped her child a time or two to the point where she's basically done the report for her child? I'm guilty. Please hear my heart here. I'm not saying helping is bad. I'm saying that when we step in so much and so often that the resounding message to our child is they are incapable, that's dangerous.

"The…destructive…message is that the parents don't trust their children to do what they are supposed to do whether it be learning to fall asleep on their own, figuring out how to safely climb a tree, or remembering to do the homework assignment. This message is especially harmful. Children cannot believe in themselves if the most important people in their lives don't believe in them."[1]

Many of the articles I read on overparenting warned that kids who grow up with a hovering parent are at higher risk for anxiety disorders and depression. They are also more likely to meander after college, where they lead a less directed and controlled life that should have been theirs as youngsters. Not to mention that parenting this way causes anxiety, stress, and can be completely draining. So much focus is placed on the child that not only does the mom suffer, but the marriage suffers. Sadly, the child's relationship with the father, who has been sent the message that he's the assistant—not the real capable parent—also suffers.[2]

At the other end of this spectrum are those who proudly call themselves "slacker moms." It's not that these parents don't care. On the contrary. They care about relationships, not activities. Muffy Mead-Ferro, author of *Confessions of a Slacker Mom,* said in a recent interview, "When it comes to parenting, often less is more." Her book and her life are all about opting out of the "frenzied competition of modern parenting." Mead-Ferro has yet to drive either child to a music lesson or soccer game. "She says she has been too busy doing things such as continuing her career in advertising; the children have been too busy doing things like playing in the backyard."[3]

I believe some mothers are driving themselves to the brink of insanity by signing their children up for everything from traveling soccer to violin lessons to SAT prep-camp to private Harvardlike preschools to tutors to manners classes to dance class to the one play date her calendar would allow...and that's just one child's schedule. Her other kids have their own laundry list of activities. I saw a cartoon once that perfectly illustrated this kind of childhood. Two preschool kids are talking on the playground, each holding their palm pilots. After reviewing each of their overcrowded schedules, they finally decide on a date months down the road.

But being a full-fledged slacker mom is a tough pill to totally swallow. These moms don't sign their kids up for activities at all. They send them outside to play. This sounds great unless you have a child who really seems gifted at a particular skill and loves doing it. How can I tell my daughter who loves gymnastics and who is excelling in this sport that I don't want the hassle of driving her to and from practice day after day? She should just go outside and play. How do I tell my teenage sons that they can't play on the school basketball team, though they're both athletically inclined and it is healthy for them to participate? With good conscience, I can't do that.

So what is a mom to do? I am taking an honest evaluation of what is realistic and necessary for my family and finding balance for the journey. None of my kids are on the fast track to Harvard, but none of them are flunking out of school, either. Now, if we had an Einstein in our midst, I would certainly foster this gift. If I had a kid who simply could not function in a traditional school setting, we'd make necessary changes. Balance. Doing what you can with what you've been given based on what is realistic.

I say we take what is good about the supermom to see if there is anything realistic that she does that fits in with the unique needs of our children. Then we take the relaxed, stress-free attitude of the slacker mom and honestly assess what we are doing too much of and seek to create a little more white space in our families. Hey, Mom, let's start a new group of mothers called the "realistic moms." Oh, but that doesn't start with an *s*...how slacker. Then again, at least we have a title...how super.

Refresh My Soul

Read Psalm 31:6; 40:4.

When you think about idols, what do you picture? A golden calf? A statue of a big, fat Buddha? Idols aren't only carved from gold or silver. They are more often carved within the depths of our hearts. They look a lot like the things we hold dear—even our children can be idols. An idol is anything that gets in the way of our relationship with God or anything that becomes more important than Him in our lives. Psalm 44:20-21 says, "If we had forgotten the name of our God or spread out our hands to a foreign god, would not God have discovered it, since He knows the secrets of the heart?"

Think about the activities and pursuits your family is involved in. How important are achievements to you? Where does God fit in the time you spend ferrying your children around? Be honest with yourself in assessing your involvement with your kids. Do you need for them to succeed so you can feel like a better mom? Is your identity associated with their success? God is aware of the secrets of our hearts—even the ones we can't admit to ourselves. As our Creator, He knows us intimately. He can help us to search our hearts and determine any changes we should make in our lives. He can shine a light into our hearts in the darkest places, and open our eyes to His desires for us. Spend some time in prayer about your priorities, and ask God to reveal to you any idols in your life you might not be aware of.

There is such comfort in turning to the Lord. As the verses you read tell us, place your trust in Him and you will be blessed (Psalm 40:4). "O LORD Almighty, blessed is the man [or mom] who trusts in you" (Psalm 84:12). Do you want to receive God's blessings? Do you want your children to receive God's blessings? Then place your trust in Him. Ecclesiastes 1:14 says that man's pursuit of the things of this world "are meaningless, a chasing after the wind." Do you place your trust in the things of this world or in the God of this world? Busyness, chasing after achievements, and filling our days with man-made idols will leave us feeling empty and breathless. We must fill our days with a rich relationship with God in order to feel fulfilled.

How can you place your trust in Him? By committing the things of your life to prayer. By seeking His will for your life and your children's lives. By doing away with anything that stands in the way of drawing closer to Him. By living a life of radical obedience and having a "yes heart" for God. As you begin to implement these elements in your life, you will find that "the things of earth will draw strangely dim," as the old hymn says. When that happens, nothing will be more important to you than pursuing Him.

12

Boundaries, Please

*How we spend our days is, of
course, how we spend our lives.*

ANNIE DILLARD

I love my little Jack Russell terrier named Champ, but let me
assure you, he had some serious boundary issues when we
first got him. We loved him and he knew it. But for some reason,
though he seemed to love us, he loved to run away more. It
became so bad that we could hardly open the front door without
him bolting for freedom. It broke my heart to see him running
wildly and carefree from our home. He had no idea of the dangers
of speeding cars, poisons that can be found in many garages,
and bigger dogs who could eat him for lunch. A fence was out
of the question. We live on 12 acres of land. And I thought the
shock collar fences were very cruel. So we just kept trying to
train him to stay.

The first night that I had to go to bed having not found him
yet, I was an absolute basket case. I had a fitful night of sleep

full of nightmares of all that could happen to my beloved pup. I kept having visions of him lying in a ditch on the side of the road somewhere. I cried. I prayed. I paced. I cried and prayed some more. Then miraculously, he found his way home the next morning. I was so relieved and overjoyed. But the celebration was short-lived, as he ran away again the next week. And the next. And the next.

Our dog's bad habit became a constant prayer request at our church. Silly, I admit, but we loved this crazy dog, so we and our friends prayed often. Even our pastor was aware of the situation. As he was driving home after a Wednesday night service, he called me on my cell phone to tell me he'd just found Champ. I couldn't believe he could have broken free from the chain we'd secured him with in the front yard or that he could have run that far from home. But as the pastor described Champ in perfect detail, I felt my blood boil.

I fumed all the way to meet the pastor in a nearby school parking lot. As I got out of the car and started to scold my wayward pooch, I became horrified as I realized this was not Champ! His markings were the same, but it definitely was not our Jack Russell.

Oh my stars, my pastor kidnapped someone else's dog! I was shocked. He was shocked. The poor Champ look-alike was shocked. And I'm sure the owner who watched my pastor drive off with her dog was really shocked! It was finally time for Champ to get a shock of his own. We called the Invisible Fence Company. Champ needed some boundaries, and a shock collar would help keep him accountable.

Moms can learn a lot from Champ. While I'm not saying we need shock collars (though I've often thought they might come in handy with wayward children...just kidding!), I do think moms need boundaries. The demands on mothers seem to be never ending, but even the best athletes require a time-out every now and then. So do we. Whether we lean more toward being a slacker mom, supermom, or realistic mom, the reality is we need to give ourselves permission to stop being a mom for a while and just be a woman...a wife...a friend.

I can't tell you how many moms I've met who pride themselves on having never left their children for any reason. They put everything on the back burner in the name of being mom extraordinaire. If this is you, please know I'm not being critical or judgmental. You know your kids and your unique situation. I'm just giving you something important to think about. If you don't take care of yourself and give yourself permission to get refreshed and refilled, don't be surprised when you constantly feel drained and secretly resentful of your family. I've seen moms who become so drained from the everyday stresses of motherhood that they seem to snap one day and run away from their responsibilities.

I've also seen moms who have never known how to embrace the joys of motherhood and seek to simply squeeze being a mom into an already overcrowded life. While these women don't physically abandon their children, they check out emotionally and spiritually. They are swept away in a world of putting the raising of their kids on caretakers and teachers. Instead of facing their children's issues head-on, they seek to appease them for the moment. But beware. This is a very dangerous place to be.

Children long for three things when forming emotional security: love, acceptance, and stability. They don't need a parental buddy or slave. Where did we moms come up with the notion that we are supposed to be either of these? John Rosemond, conservative parenting expert, says, "Overwhelming numbers of today's kids are growing up thinking their mothers are obligated to them. Because the mother-child relationship has turned upside-down, inside-out and backward in the course of 40 years, today's child is at great risk of becoming a petulant, demanding, ungrateful brat. Unfortunately, the more petulant and demanding he becomes, the more likely it is his mother will feel she's not doing enough for him. And around and around they go, this codependent union of mother and child."[1]

A "buddy" or a "slave" cannot raise kids who are emotionally secure. Their children will have a skewed view of what love is. Love becomes what others give and do for them, rather than what they give and do for others. Acceptance becomes tolerance for any and all behavior in the name of not harming the child's fragile psyche. The sad thing is that if children do not learn to properly behave, while they may be tolerated by their parents, they will not be by the world at large. Unruly children become unruly adults who are set up for a disappointing and rough life journey. Finally, along with healthy love and acceptance, stability is also essential for emotional security. Stability is only possible when a solid foundation of what is right and wrong is taught and enforced. Blurred rules inconsistently carried out based on a child's emotional responses is like shifting sand. The rules in a child's life need to be established, taught, and enforced with consistency.

Setting boundaries in your child's life has many positive benefits: emotional security for your children and emotional sanity for you. Give yourself permission to claim authority over your children. Give yourself a break when you need it. Take time to be a woman, a wife, a friend, and a balanced mom. Putting these things in place will restore emotional order to your home and help you not feel so drained all the time.

And whatever happened to Champ? Yes, he was shocked a few times while learning his boundaries. But it only took a few times. Now he happily runs and plays within the boundaries set for him. He is safe and well cared for. He now knows who is boss and is more obedient than ever. He is a poster dog for canine emotional security.

Refresh My Soul

Read Psalm 62.

Do you struggle with worrying about your children? In this psalm, David encourages us to put our trust in God alone and not in our own abilities. He tells us to rest in the Lord: rest in Him when fear for our children tries to take rule, rest in Him when stress mounts in our homes, rest in Him when we want to react in anger, rest in Him when the pressures of our to-do list causes panic in our hearts, rest in Him when we question ourselves, rest in Him when our precious children don't turn out the way we had in mind. Rest.

Perhaps you are saying to yourself, "All that rest sounds good, but I'd settle for a good night's sleep!" May I encourage you to make your sleep a matter of prayer? God wants to meet our needs. He designed us to need sleep, yet we often lose sleep by worrying. We worry about the things we need to get done, about the future, and about angry words we spoke. Worry can rob us of precious physical rest. Read Deuteronomy 33:12 and Psalm 127:2. Don't lie awake consumed with worries. When you find yourself up in the night, pray. Ask God to give you sleep according to the words of Psalm 127:2. Give all of your worries to Him and exchange them for peaceful sleep.

Read Matthew 11:28-30.

How can we find rest? By coming to Jesus. Jesus longs to give us the rest we desire. He longs to comfort us, to reassure us, to take us off the wheel we are frantically running on and grant us rest for our souls—spiritual rest. Understand that spiritual rest will renew you in a way that physical rest never can. Spiritual rest will provide emotional strength and peace deep within you. When our souls are rested, our physical limitations are less overwhelming. Jesus promises us that His yoke is light and easy to bear. Doesn't that sound like the relief you long for? Take a few moments to pray right now and ask Jesus to take away your burdens. Specifically name the things that are weighing on you. Make it a practice to come before Him and offer up your burdens—exchanging His easy yoke for your heavy one. Thank Him for offering this to you and giving you rest. Claim the rest He offers today.

Read John 10:10.

Satan desires to rob us of our rest and keep us in a frantic state. He wants us to believe that rest is not possible. He wants us to worry and lose sleep. By doing all these things, he can make us ineffective as wives, mothers, and servants of God. When worry for your children creeps in, go back to the truth found in God's Word.

While a few prayers and some time in the Bible may not immediately solve life's problems, they will give you that peace that passes all understanding (Philippians 4:7). This is the peace offered to us by Jesus. In this life, we will always have worries—it is what we do in response to them that makes all the difference.

13

No More Mommy Guilt

*Peace is not the absence of conflict but
the presence of creative alternatives
for responding to conflict.*

DOROTHY THOMPSON

My knuckles turned white as I gripped the steering wheel and blinked back tears. I was as mad as a hornet driving to teach the Marriage and Family Sunday school class at my church. What could I possibly say to encourage others when I felt so discouraged myself?

Art had left before me when it became apparent that I was not going to be ready on time; driving to church separately made me even more upset. But I practiced my best fake smile and carefully constructed the mask I would wear to fool everyone into thinking I was just fine. I arrived at church 15 minutes late, took a deep breath, smiled, and walked into the class my husband was already in the middle of teaching.

I had no sooner sat down when one of our class members got out of her seat to come and give me a hug. She whispered, "We are so glad you are here. Art told us what happened, bless your heart."

BLESS MY HEART? BLESS MY HEART? That's something we Southerners say to negate the fact we just talked ugly about someone. As in, "What happened to her hair, bless her heart." Or, "She just loves to try and sing, bless her heart." No, please, don't bless my heart. I sank into my chair. I could not believe my husband just shared how our morning had gone. My mask was shattered. The truth was out. Everyone now knew I was a gold star member of the Mommy Guilt Club.

The morning had held such promise. I'd spent the weekend switching out the kids' summer clothes to prepare for the cooler weather now upon us. I made a mental inventory of who needed what and hit the sales racks at several stores to complete everyone's wardrobe. This is no small task when you have five kids! But I wanted my kids to look neat, warm, clean, and somewhat matching. After all, how they look is a direct reflection of what kind of mother they have, right?

Well, I was in the midst of helping everyone decide what to wear to church that morning when the complaining started. "My shirt is too big!" "My pants are too tight." "This sweater is too scratchy." "I'm not wearing these striped tights. They are totally uncool." Yesterday the kids were thrilled with their new clothes. Everything fit, felt fine, and looked cool. Now nothing worked.

I went from feeling like mother of the year with well-dressed kids to the defeated and deflated mother of a ragtag-looking bunch. The kids were frustrated, I was mad, and my husband was threatening to make his children wear their worn-out summer clothes through the winter. And now it's time for church—skippidee do dah day! Art left for church with the kids, armed with a newfound prayer request.

How could things have gone so wrong? Why was I so upset? Why did I even care about whether my kids had on clothes that kept them warm and matched? It wasn't that cold, and no one would be handing out fashion demerits at church that day. I was tripped up again by mommy guilt. This is a strange phenomena that plagues many mothers, myself included.

So I've decided to claim, "No more mommy guilt!" and thought you might want to join me. Here are some of our new rules:

1. I will no longer be fooled into thinking that my kids came to me good and anything bad they do is a reflection of my poor mothering. No, kids are bad when they come to us. They have the same sin nature that causes you and me to sin, and they need a Savior just as much as we do. How else do you explain that sometimes great parents have a rotten child and rotten parents have a great child? I mean, even God, the perfect parent, had Adam and Eve, who had to be sent to the most serious time-out of them all...all the way out of the Garden! Therefore, instead of pointing the finger at myself when they act bad or make poor choices, I will point them toward their heavenly Father. I will assess what correction the kids need and administer that, but I will not let my kids' poor choices define me as a mother.

2. I will have the courage to let them live with the consequences of their bad choices. This is tough because we moms have become masters at fixing and arranging and protecting, which is necessary when they are very young. But at some point we have to start shifting responsibility to them. We want the best for our kids and think all our extra efforts to fill in their gaps are a good thing, but it isn't. Next Sunday I'm going to announce when I'm leaving for church and what the temperature is for that day. When it's time to go, we'll go. If they don't match, then I'll just let one of their peers break the news to them. If they're cold, too bad. I'll bet they'll remember a jacket next week. But I will not follow behind my children for the rest of their lives, picking up the pieces of their bad choices.

3. I'm going to stop feeling guilty over telling my kids no. I already tell my kids no quite a bit, but I often feel guilty for doing so. Well, not anymore. "No" is a great answer

and one they will hear for the rest of their lives from other people. Why shouldn't they go ahead and get used to hearing it from me now? As long as I balance the nos with enough yes answers to keep their hearts from getting discouraged, hearing no will be good for them. Sometimes my kids will have to accept my no without an explanation. Other times, I will use my no as a teachable moment. I am going to arm myself with plenty of good solid reasons and Scripture verses to back up why I'm saying no. Either way, I like the sound of this liberating word...no, no, no.

4. I will not compare myself to the seemingly perfect moms I know. Look, motherhood is hard. Seventy percent of mothers will admit to having struggles with this complicated role, and I'm convinced the other 30 percent simply aren't telling the truth. We all have good days and bad days, good moments and bad moments, victories and defeats. Just as there are no perfect children, there are no perfect mothers. We are all just doing the best we can. We all need to call out to God often for strength, courage, wisdom, patience, and grace, grace, grace. Instead of criticizing each other, we moms should band together, encourage one another, and help each other out.

Well, these are just a few of my new rules. I'm going to continue this list and slay this beast called mommy guilt. If you bump into me in the aisles of Wal-Mart this week and my kids are wearing bathing suits in the dead of winter, just high-five me as we proudly proclaim together, "No more mommy guilt!"

Refresh My Soul

Read Psalm 38:4.

Has guilt overwhelmed you at times in your life? Mommy guilt is unique because it is so readily available if you choose to take part in it. There is so much to feel guilty about. That illness that you thought was nothing but was actually an ear infection. That jacket your child needed but you forgot to grab. The laundry you did not get to so your kids have no clean socks. And that just includes the little daily things. It does not include the big stuff—the fight your child witnessed between you and your husband, the ugly things you said to them in anger, the gaping holes in your own character that motherhood has brought out in an undeniable way. How much will they have to share on the psychiatrist's couch because of you?

Be free, my friend! Unload that overwhelming burden of guilt. I want to spend some time looking at the words "overwhelm" and "burden" in the Bible and see what God has to say about them.

First, let's look at "overwhelm." Read Psalm 40:12. Write down key phrases that stand out to you in this verse. What words describe how it feels to be overwhelmed by guilt?

David wrote these words when he was feeling overwhelmed by guilt over sin. When we feel guilt over a sin, it's because the Holy Spirit is convicting us. But when we feel guilt over something that is out of our control (for example, our children) that is usually Satan using guilt to cripple us. How should we respond?

Read Psalm 40:13-17 for David's response. Write down key responses you see in this passage.

Now let's look at "burden." Read Numbers 11:14. Have you ever felt this way as a mom? I know I have. Moses is crying out to God in this verse for relief from his burden.

Read Numbers 11:16-17. God responded by giving Moses other people to share the load.

Jesus understood the burdens we carry. Read Luke 11:46. Are you letting the influence of others make you feel guilty?

Think back to the responses you just read—David's response of calling out to God and God's response of giving Moses help. How should you respond to the burden of mommy guilt based on these Scriptures? Write down any steps you feel led to take.

Jesus' purpose in coming was to free us from guilt so that we could stand in God's presence. He said, "My yoke is easy and my burden is light" (Matthew 11:30). He wants us to have "life to the full" (John 10:10), not walk around weighted down by burdens.

Read Isaiah 6:7; Hebrews 10:19-25.

I hope reading these passages will give you confidence in Christ and that you will be free from the overwhelming burden of guilt in your life. Spend some time today asking God to renew your outlook so that you may see your children without the stain of guilt tainting your view.

"It is for freedom that Christ has set us free. Stand firm, then, and do not let yourselves be burdened again by a yoke of slavery" (Galatians 5:1).

14

Calling All Recruits

*As a remedy against all ills—poverty,
sickness, and melancholy—only one thing is
absolutely necessary: a liking for hard work.*

CHARLES BAUDELAIRE

I can still remember the Saturday morning routine as though it were yesterday. My mom and stepdad believed in instilling a good work ethic in their children. I had to get up, clean the kitchen, blow the leaves from the sidewalk, the driveway, and the back deck, and then help my mom with my little sisters. I thought it was so unfair that I had to do chores. Not many of my friends had chores. Why did I get such a bum deal to be born into a family whose parents made their children work?

To make matters worse, I had a strict curfew that was earlier than most of my friends'. My mom never bought sugar cereal and made us eat healthily. My parents made me save up my own money to buy my first car. They wouldn't let me date until I was 16, and they had to meet the guy first. And I had to earn my own spending money. I thought I had the lamest parents on the planet.

Now fast-forward to my high school reunion. Amazing what the years do to people. Amazing what a few years did to my perspective. Many of those kids that I thought had it made in high school had made little of their lives since we graduated. Back in high school, these were the kids who did not have a strict curfew. They did not have to work. They were given a car when they turned 16. Most had never been required to do any kind of chores. But now, the realities of life seemed to have hit these people a little hard. Several had dropped out of college and still had not found direction for their lives. A few still lived at home. Several had been married and divorced. Many were in debt and struggling financially.

While there are no sure things or perfect formulas in parenting, I believe that making your kids work and understand the value of a dollar is key to their future success. I now appreciate my parents' rules and have implemented them in my own home. There are times my kids don't like them anymore than I did as a kid, but they will appreciate them one day.

Recently, my teenage son Jackson was telling me how wonderful it will be when he gets to move out and get his own place. I just smiled because I knew it was his way of expressing his dislike of some of our family rules. What a bummer for him to have to do dishes every Monday, help unload and put away groceries, mow the grass, rake and blow the leaves, wash the cars, and help care for the family dog. What a bummer that his parents believe the secret to keeping teenage boys in line is to work them hard enough to get all that testosterone aggression out of them. What a bummer that he can't see PG-13 movies, even though he's well past 13. What a bummer that he has to save up his money to help buy his clothes and pay for the things he wants. What a bummer that some of his friends' parents don't have these same rules. What a bummer that he has to keep his own checking account and sit down with his dad once a month to go over his income, his bills, his tithe, and how to keep it all balanced. Oh, the hardship of it all.

Yes, one day he will have a place of his own and he won't have to do Monday dishes for the family. Chances are he'll have to dishes every day of the week and cook on top of that. Chances are he won't have to unload the groceries someone else purchased. He'll have to shop for, purchase, and put his own groceries away. Chances are he won't have to wash the car he gets chauffeured around in. He'll have his own car that will take him to and from his job. And he'll be working too much to worry about things like movies, buying clothes at the mall with his friends, or what time his friend's curfew is. And then as he sits down without his dad to balance his account, chances are he'll appreciate his parents who were so hard on him—just the way I do.

Benjamin Franklin said, "The easiest way to hold on to your shirt is to roll up your sleeves." How true. So why do we moms sometimes resist having our kids help around the house? I have talked to some moms who struggle with making their kids work. They don't want to deal with their children's resistance. They wonder how to make it fair between kids of different ages. I don't struggle with either of these issues. My thought is that it is a privilege and an honor to live in the TerKeurst home. They don't struggle with watching me work, so I'm surely not going to struggle with watching them work.

My struggle with chores wasn't whether or not the kids should do them, but whether or not they could do them well. This took training and training took time. I solicited the help of my ultraorganized husband and together we listed out the chores we needed the kids to help with. He then arranged them on an Excel spreadsheet and posted it in our kitchen. Then we tackled the job of preparing the children for each assigned task.

When training the kids, we used a method similar to the way my husband's restaurant trains their new employees:

- tell them

- show them

- work beside them

- supervise them

- inspect them

- thank them

First, we tell them what the job is and what our expectations are. Then we show them the tools they will need for the job, how to use the tools, how to accomplish the task set before them, and how to clean and store the tools for later use. After that, we work beside them, only stepping in to offer advice or lend a hand as needed. This can all be accomplished on the first day of training. The next time the child is to do this job, you supervise. Let the child do the task without you stepping in. If they have questions, answer them by reminding them of the exact procedure you covered in the original training. Afterward, praise them for all they did right, point out anything they could do a little better, and thank them for a job well done. At this point they should be ready to do the job by themselves next time. Be diligent about doing routine inspections when the kids complete their chores. You don't have to do this every time, but do it enough to hold them accountable for a job well done. This takes an initial time investment on your part. It takes some up-front thought and work, but what a worthwhile investment it has been for us. There is such freedom that comes from sharing the load of chores that are inevitable in a household with seven bodies.

Here are a few more things to consider. One of the most important is the age appropriateness of the chores you assign to your kids, as there are safety issues with chemicals and tools that can be dangerous if not handled properly. Moms with younger children should find chores that little ones can do to cast a vision for the importance of contributing to the family early in their life. Go online and type in "chores for kids" and you'll find lists and charts for kids of all ages. My youngest child matches socks, stacks plastic bowls, puts away utensils (all except the sharp knives), feeds the dog, throws the ball for the dog, helps with weeding the yard, and cleans her room.

Also keep in mind picking the right time to train them. A friend of mine made it a summer project to train each of her kids. She found this to be a slower, less scheduled time where she could really spend time implementing a system that works for her family.

Finally, remember that attitude is everything. Teach your children to keep a happy heart while they work by modeling it. Play some happy music, catch your children having a great attitude while they work, reward them with a special prize, and always remember to praise them for a job well done.

By the way, we don't pay our kids to help with the everyday chores: kitchen duty, dog duty, pool duty, laundry duty, and keeping their rooms and bathrooms clean. The chores on our chore chart are a requirement for living in our home. We do, however, give the kids an opportunity to earn money with extra jobs. The boys get paid extra to do yard work or help their dad with special projects. The girls get paid extra for cleaning the vehicles or helping me with special projects.

The point is, give your children the gift of a good work ethic. It is a gift that will bless you in the short-term and reap rich dividends for them in the long-term.

Refresh My Soul

Read Psalm 128.

This passage describes God's perfect design for a home and family. In verse 2, we read, "You will eat the fruit of your labor."

Now read Genesis 3:17.

Part of the consequence of Adam's sin was to work hard for his food for the rest of his life. Since then, all men have had to work to eat—either by growing crops and raising animals or by earning the money to buy food and necessities. Though God's original plan did not require this, it is the consequence of sin and part of the reality of life in a fallen world.

Were you taught to work hard as a child? If so, are you thankful now? If not, do you wish you had been raised with a stronger work ethic? What would you like to teach your kids about work? Write down your thoughts on this.

Read 1 Corinthians 4:12; Philippians 2:14; Colossians 3:23; 2 Thessalonians 3:10.

Based on these verses, what does the Bible have to say about work? Use these verses to help you teach your children. When they complain or argue about doing chores, go back to these Scriptures. Help them to see that hard work and contributing to the family is a part of life. It will develop their character and it pleases God. Remind them often that they are honoring God when they participate in daily chores. If you decide to create a chore chart, consider adding one or two of these verses to the chart as a "friendly reminder" of the attitude they should have about work.

Read 1 Corinthians 11:1; 1 Timothy 4:12; Titus 2:7-8.

What example are you setting for your kids about working? Do your kids see you working around the house—going the extra mile to create an orderly, cozy home for them? Do they see you do everything as unto the Lord? Do they see you grumble and complain about the daily tasks required of you? I know my kids have certainly seen me fall short of this in our home. I do try to set the standard by upholding the same work ethic I expect of them and working alongside of them. We are a family that plays together, prays together, and works together. I want my kids to know that whatever I expect of them, I expect of myself. You might want to think about this as you consider what your expectations for your children are. It is up to us to set the standard for our families. Our attitude about work will set the tone for the way our kids see it.

Read Ephesians 4:15-16.

The body of Christ is being described here, but these verses also depict an accurate picture of how a Christian family should look—each member contributing to the best of his or her ability for the good of the family. Spend time thinking of ways you can involve your kids and inspire them to work toward the good of your family. Ask God to help you think of creative ways to do so—and don't forget to think of some creative incentives while you are at it.

15

How in the World Do You Do What You Do?

What is home? A roof to keep out the rain. Four walls to keep out the wind. Floors to keep out the cold. Yes, but home is more than that.

It is the laugh of a baby, the song of a mother, the strength of a father. Warmth of living hearts, light from happy eyes, kindness, loyalty, comradeship. Home is first school and first church for young ones, where they learn what is right, what is good, and what is kind. Where they go for comfort when they are hurt or sick. Where joy is shared and sorrow eased. Where fathers and mothers are respected and loved. Where children are wanted. Where the simplest food is good enough for kings because it is earned. Where money is not as important as lovingkindness. Where even the tea kettle sings from happiness. That is home. God bless it.

MADAME ERNESTINE SCHUMANN-HEINK

When people find out I have five kids, write books, and run a ministry, their first question is always how in the world do I do all that? First of all, let me assure you there are always plenty of things I don't get finished. There are always more items on my to-do list than I ever get done. On top of that, I always underestimate the amount of time it will take to get something accomplished. But I do like having a plan to get things done, I am a good delegator, and I've made peace with the balance between my calling and my responsibilities. That's how I do what I do.

Have a Plan

The first part of a plan is to decide what to say yes to and what to say no to. It is not realistic for me to say yes to everything, so I've learned the great art of saying no. For example, I can only go to my office one day a week. While the ideal thing might be to go to the office five days a week, this is not my season for the office to take the ideal place in my life. Some days my kids are my ideal. Some days a hurting friend is my ideal. Some days my husband is my ideal. Wherever my energies need to be placed, saying no to some things gives me the ability to get intentional with the things I need to say yes to.

Once you get your "no" items out of the way, the next step is to properly schedule the things you've said yes to. We have a rule in our home that each kid can pick one outside activity to participate in. With five kids, this still equals a lot of scheduling, driving, and watching, but this is what we've decided is realistic and fair for our family. I've found it helpful to have a scheduling session with my husband once a quarter to plan out our master family calendar. Then, once each week, Art and I sit down and go over who is responsible for each of the balls being juggled that week.

Communicating ahead of time helps us avoid the pitfalls of anger, frustration, and last-minute debates as to who is running what carpool. We each have a plan. In addition to scheduled activities, the kids also put in their requests for get-togethers with friends and other social events. They know if they don't get their request in before the planning meeting, Mom and Dad have no obligation to make it happen. We not only schedule the kids' activities, but we also plan out time for us to connect. If there is time for a date night, then we write it in on the schedule. If it's a particularly busy week, we might just schedule time for coffee or a movie night at home together. Finally, we fill in our individual appointments and obligations. This is where I leave space for ministry work, doctor's appointments, orthodontist appointments, and volunteer obligations. It's much easier to know when to schedule these if you have clearly defined white space in your calendar. If there is a special project I need to accomplish, I break it down into bite-sized pieces and assign myself parts of the task each day. Some examples of special projects are a closet that needs to be organized, files that need to be updated, photographs that need to be developed and put in albums, or an area of the house that needs to be dejunked with the excess going to charity. Once all of this is in place, I feel the freedom to plan time for me in my schedule. If I want to have coffee with a friend or go on a girl's night out, I can easily see when it is realistic to make this happen.

Getting my schedule out of my brain and onto a calendar drastically reduces my stress and alleviates the feeling that my schedule is running me rather than the other way around.

Become a Good Delegator

If you cannot get everything done that is required of you, then you have to take an honest assessment with a solution in mind. My solution is to ask for help. I divide my tasks into three categories:

- Only I can do this.

- Someone else can do it under my guidance.

- I can hand this off to someone else freely.

Knowing the difference between these three categories is life-transforming! The first, only I can do this, are obviously those things only I can do. No one else can spend time with the Lord for me. No one else can make the type of emotional investments necessary to be an effective wife and mom for my family. No one else can exercise for me (oh, how I wish they could!). No one else can write my books for me. This first category contains things I make time for by giving other tasks away.

The second category are things that someone else can do under my guidance. The important thing here is to clearly communicate your expectations to the person you are giving a task to and train them to do the job the way you want it done. Once you've trained this person and they have learned the job, you can then hand off this task to them freely. The time you invest on the front end training and educating on the right way to accomplish a task will reap great benefits on the back end.

This is where my kids come in. There are lots of household tasks the children are perfectly capable of handling. (See chapter 14, "Calling All Recruits," for more ideas.) Also, I have a sitter who helps me run my afternoon carpools. Art and I have decided it is better to give up other things to have the finances to make this possible for my sanity's sake.

Are there tasks in your life that can be delegated to others? Are you willing to ask your husband and kids for help? Do you need to look outside your home for a helper who can take on some of the things that might be bogging you down?

Another creative solution is to look for a homeschool helper to be the person to whom you are delegating. I found a family of teenaged homeschool girls who were looking to make some extra money. They come help me with whatever chores I can't get done on my own. They help with laundry, dishes, organizing kids' rooms, and whatever else I put on their list. I love the help. They love the spending money, and they even earn school credits for home economics. Pray about a creative solution if you are looking for some help. God will hear your prayer and help you know to whom and how to delegate.

Make Peace with the Balance Between Calling and Responsibilities

As moms, we must stop looking around for validation and affirmation of what kind of mother we are to be. We can't look to our friends. We can't look to our parents. We can't look at and compare ourselves to other moms. We must stop looking around and start looking up. God will be faithful to reveal His individual plan for you.

> But how do we act on the God-given purposes in our lives and still be attentive, caring wives and mothers? First, we abandon the idea that God has designed life so family is separate from service and that the two must compete. In a speech at the 1997 Women's Ministries Symposium, Jill Briscoe talked about the fallacy of having a hierarchy of priorities, such as (1) God, (2) husband, (3) children, (4) church, and so on. Instead, she suggested, there's a hierarchy of principles—"God and his kingdom come first. God will tell you what is front and center today. Are you listening?" If you're a praying person who listens to God and looks into the hearts of people around you, obeying the first and second commandments to love God and love others (Matthew 22:37-39), you'll know when to skip the day's entire to-do list and take your kids to the beach, take yourself to the beach, take your Bible to the beach, or take your kids and your neighbor's lonely, autistic son to the beach…Contrary to what some people may believe, a woman doesn't have to choose between having a purpose in life and being a faithful and fun-loving mom, wife, and friend. One of the best things we can contribute to the people we love is to be a woman who responds to the call of God. Through us, those we love experience the joy of following God and are often challenged to consider their own God-infused purposes."[1]

A calling on a woman's life will be unique and personal. God knows your husband better than you. God knows your children better than you. He knows what kind of wife and mom they need. He knows what kind of demands will be required of you in every role you play. So turn each day over to Him and let Him order your steps. Ask Him where to start, take that step, and then ask what is the next step you are to take. All the while pray that your spiritual eyes and ears will be open and attentive to any pit stops along the way God might have for you.

Having a plan, learning to delegate, and making peace with your calling will help you get done what needs to be accomplished and get more intentional with those you love.

Refresh My Soul

Read Psalm 121.

Where does your help come from?

You have just had a glimpse of my life and how I do what I do. In this chapter, I wanted to provide you with an opportunity to honestly assess and investigate what you do by answering this most popular of questions. While I offered practical and logistical tips in this chapter, I want to spend a few moments here encouraging you to first and foremost seek help from the Lord. In all I have learned about making my life work for me, this has been my greatest lesson. I must find my true help in Him.

In verse 2 of this psalm, the psalmist identifies God as "the LORD, the Maker of heaven and earth." He is the God of the universe, the Creator of all things.

Read Psalm 96:10-13.

All things fall under the authority of God. As their Creator, they all must obey according to His will. This order and authority brings me great peace and comfort. I know that nothing happens in my life that has not been first filtered through the hands of God. For this reason, I have learned to view what could be seen as life's interruptions as opportunities instead. Each day I submit my plans, my ideas, and my desires to His ultimate authority. This is what brings me joy and makes my life work, no matter what. I can call on God for help because He is in control.

Read Psalm 33:6-11.

This is a beautiful passage about God's authority over all creation. Verse 11 tells us that "the plans of the LORD stand firm forever, the purposes of his heart through all generations." This means that His purpose extends into the generations to come. Your children and grandchildren will be affected and shaped by His purposes as well. You are leaving a legacy by learning to respond to His plans for you.

Proverbs 19:21 says, "Many are the plans in a man's heart, but it is the LORD's purpose that prevails."

What are your plans? Are there things in your life that aren't going according to your plans? Take comfort in knowing and accepting that—for whatever reason—God has allowed this as part of His purposes for you.

Now, reread Psalm 121:3-8.

These verses are here to encourage you today. God knows you intimately. He knows what you are facing. He knows the details of your life. These verses tell us that He watches over your life. He watches your coming and going. (Wow! That means God sees all those trips to soccer practice and runs to the grocery store.) Even when you sleep, God is taking care of things because He does not sleep. Allow these verses to seep into your heart and become part of your thought life. The God of the universe cares for you! He is there to help you release what you don't need to be doing and give you strength to do the rest.

16

Little Comforts of Refreshment

*A little nonsense, now and then, is
cherished by the wisest men.*

ROALD DAHL

A special tradition in our home is an afternoon treat. A nutritionist may or may not agree with me, but I think it's a *heart*-healthy habit. Not that our treats are always that healthy, mind you. My kids and I love fresh-baked cookies, chewy brownies, and other concoctions of all kinds. Sometimes we eat apples, oranges, or some other snack from the healthier regions of the food pyramid, but mostly we like a sweet treat.

These treats are "heart" healthy for how they create moments of joy amid busy schedules, projects that are due, activities to attend, and chores to be done. They are little bursts of comfort that I, as a mom, delight in giving my children. They say "I love you...I think about ways to make you happy...and I consider it a privilege to enjoy a treat with you."

I remember my mom making gingersnap cookies for me when I was a little girl. How those cookies made me happy. Even now I can close my eyes and picture my mom rolling little balls of brown dough through sugar before placing them on a cookie sheet. Then I'd watch as she placed them in the oven. It seemed as though it took forever for them to be transformed from dough balls to puffy baked cookies. But the best part was my mom and me enjoying the first bite together. Even when I grew older and no longer took part in the baking, these treats were still connection points between my mom and me. As a teenager, I loved walking in after school and smelling the evidence of this treat floating through the air. To this day the smell of ginger makes me smile.

If these little treats made me so happy as a child, why do they have to stop? I mean, why is it that I sometimes think motherhood is all about what I do for others and never stop to think of the wonderful benefits of treating myself?

I can see the church lady from the depths of my religious background jumping out with a finger wagging. "Don't be so worldly! Pull out your Bible and read a verse or two. Get refreshed from the Spirit. Drink the Living Water and you'll never thirst again. If you are feeling really weary, sing a verse or two of 'It Is Well with My Soul' and stop thinking of yourself. It is better to give than to receive!" And with a quick huff, roll of her eyes, and shaking of her head, she turns and vanishes. Yikes! I whisper back at her, "If you are so into giving these days, I'd gladly let you watch my five kids, run their carpools, and clean and cook for me while I go sit in the tub and sing hymns and reflect on spiritual insights."

Yes, I think the best kind of refreshment is found when we go to the Lord and ask Him to fill us. But, just as giving treats to my kids makes me happy, I think our heavenly Father would like for us to receive things that make us happy as a treat from Him. There has been so much talk about the difference between joy and happiness in the Christian world that many of us shy away from happiness. Granted, none of the things on my list provide me with lasting joy, but they sure can lighten a heavy moment of feeling drained. Why not make a list of things that make you feel happy? Then, the next time you are feeling a little drained, put a little care package together for yourself and thank God for His sweet treats. Here are some of the things on my list:

- cinnamon Altoids Gum

- black gel pen—medium point

- a candle that smells of the season

- a new pair of white socks

- lemon-flavored Propel

- brownies from a box mix

- dryer sheets—fresh spring scent

- an inspirational CD

- a cup of white chocolate mocha, skim, no whip, no foam, extra hot

Thank You, God, for these treats that make my heart happy.

Another important and practical thing I do for refreshment is to make sure I always have something to look forward to. Maybe it's a date with my husband, a night out with the girls, having time to work on my scrapbook, getting my hair done in the salon, or even something as simple as taking a bubble bath after the kids are in bed. Sometimes it's a bigger thing, such as a vacation or getting to shop for something I've saved up to buy. But whatever it is, having something to look forward to is the little glimmer of better things that gets me over the hump of hard things. It's just the sparkle my heart needs when life seems full of mundane chores, whiney complaints, and yet another mess to pick up. So look up, look forward, and put something on the horizon that will make you smile.

Finally, rid yourself of "hoarder disorder." You've heard the old expression of "save the best for last." Well, I think we can succumb to this and never savor what we have. Think about the candle that cost a little too much but you just loved the way it smelled. You bought it but only burn it for company. No, no, no. Go get it right now and burn it because you like the way it smells. Just burn it for you. And while you're at it, go get a plate of the china you never use. Even if you just eat a peanut butter and jelly sandwich on it, use it to make you feel a little more special. And that nice outfit that just hangs in your closet for the once-a-year company party? Go put it on! Come on. We'll look silly together, but we're doing it in high style, with fancy china by candlelight.

A friend of mine recently shared with me that she was at a scrapbooking party where she shared her hesitancy to use her "good" stickers. A lady quipped back at her, "You've got hoarder disorder and you need to get over it. Pull those stickers out right now and use them. What in the world are you saving them for?"

How true! Do we really think when we are old and gray that there is going to be some kind of contest at the old folks' home? The announcer steps up on the rickety stage and pulls the squeaky microphone close. "Whoever has the most unburned candles, mint-condition china, and never-worn out-of-date clothes wins an extra bingo chip."

I don't want an extra bingo chip 50 years from now. I want to be a happy person. I want to be a mother with a smile on her face. I want to teach my kids that it doesn't mean you are a worldly person if you happen to find a little joy in the things of this world that bring your heart comfort.

Be refreshed, my friend. Put together a little care package of happy things for yourself. Put something on your calendar to look forward to, and don't save your best for last.

Refresh My Soul

Read Psalm 33:13-22.

Having something to look forward to—to hope for—isn't worldly thinking. It's biblical!

Read Proverbs 13:12.

If you have read any of my other books or heard me speak, you may already know that Art and I named our first daughter "Hope" because of the hope we found in our struggling marriage. We claimed Jeremiah 29:11, " 'For I know the plans I have for you,' declares the LORD. 'Plans to prosper you and not to harm you, plans to give you hope and a future.'"

Ultimately, our hope must be in the Lord. As we seek to know Him better, to trust Him with our lives, and to submit to His will, we can find peace in spite of our circumstances. We can trust that "in all things God works for the good of those that love him" (Romans 8:28).

While we can't see the beautiful tapestry He is weaving from our lives, we have hope in His sovereignty alone. "Hope that is seen is no hope at all. Who hopes for what he already has? But if we hope for what we do not yet have, we wait for it patiently" (Romans 8:24-25).

What do these verses say to you about hope?

What part does trust play in hope?

Think about your life right now. Are you waiting patiently for something you do not yet have? Perhaps it is the hope of having a child. Perhaps it is the hope of physical healing. Perhaps it is the hope of a restored marriage or financial freedom. These are things you *can* hope for with God's help.

Write down whatever your hope is. What are you looking forward to in your life?

If you cannot think of anything to write, pray that God would give you a vision of something to hope for. As a mom, it's okay to dream big. Remember what Proverbs 13:12 says about "a longing fulfilled." You were designed by God to have dreams!

Read Psalm 119:74; 1 Thessalonians 5:8; Titus 1:2.

Based on these verses, what should our hope be rooted in?

Have you ever put your hope in these things?

Spend some time in prayer today asking God to give you hope or to restore your hope. If you have not put your hope in Christ, eternal life, God's Word, and salvation, perhaps you are feeling led to do so now. Jesus longs to give you the hope your soul is crying out for. The hope of eternal life will never fail you. You can always cling to His Word. Through salvation, you will always have something to look forward to.

I will leave you with Paul's words from Romans 15:13: "May the God of hope fill you with all joy and peace as you trust in him, so that you may overflow with hope by the power of the Holy Spirit."

A Renewed Perspective

17

The Most Beautiful Scars

*I think women see me on the cover of
magazines and think I never have a
pimple or bags under my eyes. You have to
realize that that's after two hours of hair
and makeup, plus retouching. Even I don't
wake up looking like Cindy Crawford.*

Cindy Crawford

Mommy, what are those silvery lines on your hips?" Brooke
was inquiring about the stretch marks that are plentiful on
my body since birthing three of my five kids. She was studying
them with an intense curiosity mixed with great concern as to
what kind of horrible animal could have scratched and scarred
me so greatly. As I informed her about the beauty of what the
stretch marks represented to me, she couldn't get past how
unsightly they were to her.

"Good thing those marks aren't on your feet where everyone
would be able to see them," she quipped back. Again, I stressed

the fact that the stretch marks were a beautiful reminder that my body was used in a sacrificial way to make her birth and the birth of her two sisters possible. It's the mark of the ultimate servant who gives their life to make new life possible for others. Not that I actually died in the process, but the way my body looked before I had children, smooth and unblemished, died during the rigors of pregnancy. Impressed with my own answer, I replied back to her, "Now don't you think they are beautiful?"

She wasn't in tune with my spiritual correlations and clever metaphors. "Mom," she started slowly, "you are beautiful, but those marks...not so beautiful." Oh, the honesty of a six-year-old! Really, she's right in one sense. The marks themselves are not so beautiful. They are jagged, uneven, and discolored signs that my skin was stretched almost beyond what it could bear. It was stretched so thin that it will never quite be the same.

I stood before the mirror and continued to examine the stark evidence of my past pregnancies. A strange sense of pride welled up in my heart as I realized these scars made me like Jesus in a way. I gave of my life to make new life possible. I carried this new person and took on their weight. I was stretched almost beyond what I could bear. My experience left me scarred and forever marked. But the product of these scars is a joy I could not have any other way.

It still moves me to tears to think about Jesus' scars. Amazing that the God of the universe would care so much for me that He would allow His Son to give up His life for me. While I have not been called upon to physically die for my children, I have been called to die to the selfishness that characterized my life before kids. Life was about me back then. My schedule, my needs, my wants, my time, my money, my desires, my dreams, and my plans dictated how I spent my life. But that is not what God wanted for me. He wanted my life to be about Him and His plans for me. So in march not one, not two, not three, not four, but five little beings to make sure I am reminded on a daily basis that acts of service to others is what the pathway to joy is paved with. Little stones of service that, when carefully laid beside each other, lead to great places.

Braiding this one's hair. Tying this one's shoes. Fixing this one his favorite cookies. Changing this one's diaper. Taking this one out for coffee. Cheering this one at her sport's events. Praying this one through a hard time. Washing this one's clothes. Dusting this one's room. Cleaning up this one's spilled drink. Teaching this one to roller skate. Planning this one's birthday party. Helping this one catch a frog. Putting a bandaid on this one's scraped knee.

And that's just one day in the life of a mom.

I am convinced there is no greater way to model for our kids the heart of God than to serve our families with a happy heart. Not that we are to become our children's slaves. That would teach them laziness and disrespect. But to model for them the joy that can be found in giving our lives in service to our Lord and others. When we model this for our kids, we set the standard for what we expect from them. I expect my kids to have a good attitude when serving family members and others. I want for them what I have discovered—when you serve, you look at lot like Jesus.

> We give of ourselves when we give gifts of the heart—love, kindness, joy, understanding, sympathy, tolerance, forgiveness.
>
> We give of ourselves when we give gifts of the minds—ideas, dreams, purposes, ideals, principles, plans, inventions, projects, poetry.
>
> We give of ourselves when we give gifts of words—encouragement, inspiration, guidance.
>
> Emerson said it well—"Rings and jewels are not gifts, but apologies for gifts. The only true gift is a portion of thyself."[1]

Jesus gave the one true gift in the most profound way. He gave His very life so I could find new life. My scars, therefore, are precious reminders—treasures, really—of my service that started the moment of my children's conception and continues to this day. Giving of my body gave my kids a chance at life. Modeling Jesus' example of service points them to a new life they can have in Christ. They don't have to fall prey to the selfishness that reigns in this world.

I don't have to fall victim to the selfishness that screams for attention sometimes as well. I become a giving person by giving. I become a caring person by caring. I become like Jesus by acting like Jesus. Not by thinking about it, not by making promises to do it, but rather by the act itself.

Just as these acts change me permanently, my scars also are a permanent marking. Trust me, I know how permanent they are. Before I came to appreciate their beauty, I tried all kinds of creams and lotions with big promises to reduce the appearance of scars. Some products were even bold enough to claim to heal stretch marks. I became a marketing statistic as I fell prey to their empty promises. No amount of cream, no amount of rubbing, and no amount of wishing them away worked. They have become permanent residents on my hips. So, since I cannot make them disappear, I have chosen to embrace these symbols of my courageous attempt at motherhood.

Jesus embraced His scars as well. And now for all of us, they are symbols of His courageous success of becoming the Savior of the world. In His resurrection, He could have come back without the scars on His hands, feet, and side, but He left them there. The rest of His body was whole and healed, so why leave these scars? While theologians could argue this question in great debate, I think He left them because He wanted to. He came to love not the scars themselves, but what the scars accomplished. He was called to be the Savior of the world, and He did it. I am called to be a mom, and I'm doing it.

Let's face it. Motherhood is a stretching experience whether we are talking about our physical bodies, our mental capacity, or our spiritual outlook. But it brings me such joy to see the correlations between my service to my children and what Jesus has done for me that I thought it worth pondering. Whether you birthed your children through your body or through your heart through adoption, you have served…you have sacrificed…you have been stretched.

I looked at the older woman and wondered what it meant.
Do we tell with our body about the life we have spent?
The wrinkles on her face, the posture of her back.
The fingers softly bent, the joy in her laugh.
I'd seen other faces marked with a frown and scorn.
Their presence seemed quite harsh, their spirit very worn.
But in this woman was a beauty, despite the evidence of time.
Peace in her cloudy eyes and laughter behind her laugh lines.
She had a grace about her, though her body was now slow.
For she had learned the joy of being, and in her heart she knows.
She spent her life in celebration, choosing joy to be found
In whatever life gave her she stood on His solid ground.
Lord, may the markings on my body be like hers in some way
That I loved and laughed and gave and celebrated every single day.

Lysa TerKeurst

Refresh My Soul

Read Psalm 100 and record your favorite section of this passage.

In verse 2 it says to come before the Lord with joyful songs. How have you been coming to the Lord lately?

It is good to be honest with God, but we must be careful that we don't become whiners. There is nothing that aggravates my heart more than to hear whining and complaining, especially from my kids. I can't help but think the Lord might feel the same way. I have caught myself coming to Him simply with a bad attitude. Is there anything you've been having a bad attitude about lately?

Even amid hardship, trials, and things that don't go the way we want them to, we can find something to be joyful about. My stretch marks story might be a silly example of this, but it makes this point. How did this perspective encourage you?

Read 2 Corinthians 9:13.

What must accompany our profession that Christ is our Lord?

Sometimes it is easier to be obedient in our actions than our attitude. Do you need to take an honest look at any of your mothering attitudes?

The prayer that changes everything, according to Stormie Omartian, is praise. Write a prayer of praise to God regarding being a mom.

"I will walk in my house with blameless heart" (Psalm 101:2). This verse is both convicting and challenging to me. David, the author of this psalm, knew he would need God's help to have a blameless heart. There are things he encourages us to avoid throughout Psalm 101. List those things here.

Interestingly enough, all the negative things listed in this psalm affect our attitude and our desire to praise God. Are you looking at TV shows or movies that are negative and dishonoring to God? Are there people in your life who are dragging you down? Do you struggle with talking poorly about others? Are there areas of pride in your life? Take an honest evaluation of each of these questions and list your answers here.

What does it mean to walk in my house with a blameless heart?

Write your favorite line from the poem on page 137 and why it touched your heart.

18

The Truth Behind
Our Gaps

For years I stared at the stained white laminate countertops in my kitchen and dreamed of replacing them with granite. Not only were they discolored and scratched, but parts of them were buckled from water damage. Let's just say they had seen better days and it was time for them to go. It's not that I wanted fancy, expensive countertops. I wanted durable countertops that would hide dust and crumbs if I missed a few spots while wiping them down. The particular kind I wanted could even handle hot items being placed directly on their durable surface. Plus, I think granite is really pretty.

We saved for years to afford these countertops. Finally, we had enough money to remodel the kitchen. I was so excited the day I saw the laminate being ripped out and thrown away. A few days later, while I was out of town, my husband called to tell me the granite had arrived. Then he asked me which I wanted first: the good news or the bad news?

I didn't like the sound of his question at all. He assured me the granite looked very pretty, but there were sizable veins running the length of both countertops that looked like cracks. I knew just enough about granite to know it is quite common for granite to have veins. That's why I'd taken the time to go to the granite distributor and handpick my slabs. I wanted to ensure no veins. Now, according to Art, we had the exact opposite of what I'd requested. I just shook my head and told him I'd deal with it when I got home.

I spotted the cracklike veins the minute I walked into the kitchen. I quickly realized there was no good solution to this problem. It's not as though you can just pack up granite countertops, grab your receipt, and return them to the store. The installer blamed it on the dealer. The dealer blamed it on the wholesaler. The wholesaler said he'd delivered the exact lot I'd chosen. In other words, he blamed me. No one was willing to help fix the problem without a lot of headache and cost. Basically, I was going to have to deal with the cracks or spend money we didn't have to have them changed.

In a frustrated huff I sat down at the kitchen bar and stared at the ugly black lines disfiguring the beautiful countertops I'd dreamed of for years. I realized that every time I looked at the veins, it would evoke some kind of emotion. I couldn't change that. But I could change the emotion they brought forth.

I ran my hand across the black mark and prayed for God's perspective. The first thing that occurred to me was that while the vein looked like a crack, it wasn't. It was a natural occurrence that actually proved the authenticity of the granite.

That didn't make me feel any better.

The next thing that occurred to me was that the countertops were still perfectly functional. They would still be able to serve the purpose for which I wanted.

True, but that didn't make me feel any better, either.

Then I felt God's gentle voice fill my heart with His wisdom. "Any time there is a gap in your life, let your heart be drawn to Me. On this side of heaven, there will always be gaps. Life will always fall short. Each time you notice the vein in your granite, let it be a reminder that I can fill your gaps. Let it be a call to praise Me."

Though there wasn't an actual gap in the granite, there was a gap in the way it met my expectations. These types of gaps can be frustrating, bothersome, and quite draining. Your husband forgets your anniversary, a gap. Your child so desperately wants to be good at something she's clearly not good at, and you don't know how to lovingly steer her in another direction, a gap. You've promised yourself not to act so hormonal during your next bout with PMS, but in the middle of flying off the handle at something very small, you fail again, a gap. You and your husband work for hours and finally have a handle on your budget. No more unplanned spending. Then a car repair, a medical bill, and a visit to the grocery store without your list blows your budget again, a gap.

Whether it is a gap in your marriage, in your parenting abilities, in your finances, in your friendships, in your job, in your spiritual walk, or even in your countertops, God wants to reveal to you His ability to fill that gap. He wants to whisper His truths, His perspectives, and His wisdom straight to your heart. He hears your cries. He will help you handle the gap. He just wants you to remember three truths for the gaps of life:

1. Let this gap be a reminder to draw closer to God. There will always be gaps in life on this side of heaven. They remind us that this is not our real home. Our souls were created for the perfection of paradise, but our journey here on earth is riddled with potholes and mud puddles. If it weren't, then we'd have no desire for our real home. We'd become so complacent here that we wouldn't press on toward heaven. We also have to ask ourselves honestly if this gap is the result of a sinful desire waging war in our heart. If so, admit it, repent of it, and ask God to set your heart free from it. First Peter 2:11 says, "Dear friends, I urge you, as aliens and strangers in the world, to abstain from sinful desires, which war against your soul." If I can be real honest, the real problem with the gap in my countertop

was my own pride. It's a sign of imperfection, and I don't like my imperfections to show. *Lord, please set my heart free from these prideful tendencies.*

2. Having God's perspective for a gap gives you hope. This hope will glorify God and cause others to notice Christ in you. First Peter 3:15 says, "But in your hearts set apart Christ as Lord. Always be prepared to give an answer to everyone who asks you to give the reason for the hope that you have." When people ask me about the black lines that streak across my countertops, I smile as the question prepares the way for me to share Jesus. I bet most find my answer strange and unexpected. I'm sure they expect an answer full of grumbling and complaining. Instead, I tell them how the marks on my countertops remind me about the gaps in my life. I share how I depend on God to fill these. These experiences bring me joy, glorify God, and maybe cause others to think about the gaps in their lives in a little different light.

3. The gap won't be there forever. Either the gap will go away or your awareness of it will. First Peter 5:6-7 says, "Humble yourselves, therefore, under God's mighty hand, that he may lift you up in due time. Cast all your anxiety on him because he cares for you." When the granite was first installed, the veins were all I noticed, but time has a great way of letting things fade into the background. Unless someone asks about the black veins, I don't notice them any longer. They blend in with the other natural flecks and markings in the granite. They are just part of the counter-tops now. God has lifted me up past the petty worry of a marking on my kitchen countertops. There are other gaps in my life that aren't so petty that I'm still waiting to be lifted up from. But God is caring for me each and every day. As I cast my cares on Him, He releases His affections and sweeps me away from the worries of my gaps.

Go to that place in your home where a gap exists. Maybe it's a big stain on your den carpet, crayon marks down your hallway, or scratches on your floor. (I have all of these gaps too!) Ask the Lord to give you a new perspective about gaps. Be honest with God as you discuss the gaps that make you feel overwhelmed and drained at times. Let this physical reminder become a sweet sanctuary spot where you gained a new perspective from God. Be refreshed and refilled as you no longer gasp at the gaps of life.

Refresh My Soul

Read Psalm 51.

This psalm was written as a psalm of confession after David committed adultery with Bathsheba. In this psalm, David is painfully aware of his gaps and shortcomings. He knows that all he can do is fall on God's grace and ask Him to fill in his gaps in the days to come. These phrases stood out to me:

Wash away all my iniquity and cleanse me from my sin (verse 2).

Create in me a pure heart, O God, and renew a steadfast spirit within me (verse 10).

Restore to me the joy of your salvation and grant me a willing spirit, to sustain me (verse 12).

How did David respond to his gaps? How should you respond to yours?

"All have sinned and fall short of the glory of God" (Romans 3:23). We all have gaps. No one is without sin. Everyone falls short of God's perfection and His standards for us. The word "sin" actually means "missing the mark." God knows that we daily miss the mark. We might try to be perfect, but we will never be. Our only hope is in Christ.

Read Ephesians 5:25-27; Colossians 1:22.

Jesus wants to present us to God as His perfect, sinless flock. Someday that will happen when He presents us, the church, as His bride. What do these verses say about us being perfect in the eyes of God? Does this give you hope for what eternity will be like? Just think! No more gaps!

"But when perfection comes, the imperfect disappears" (1 Corinthians 13:10). In the meantime, while we wait for Christ's return, what can we do?

Where is perfection found in our lives? How can we pursue perfection?

Let me be clear. I don't mean an earthly, worldly perfection. I am not talking about outward perfection. By perfection, I mean spiritual perfection—complete communion with God. To be perfect is to be found pleasing in God's sight. This is not achieved through actions or attitude, but through a relationship with Jesus Christ. It is not something we can seek out in our flesh. Hebrews 12:2 says, "Let us fix our eyes on Jesus, the author and perfecter of our faith." Jesus authored our salvation through His death and resurrection. As we are being transformed into His image through our Christian walk, we are being perfected each day.

The only way we can hope for perfection is by following the One who is perfect.

Read Matthew 5:48; 19:21; Hebrews 10:1,14.

Write about some ways that these verses address being perfect.

Do you wish you could be the perfect wife? The perfect mom? The perfect Christian? Who hasn't wished that? I would love to rid myself of all my scratches, cracks, stains, and blemishes. I hope you will allow these verses to offer you comfort and assurance today that—while it might not be the kind of perfection you had in mind—it is possible to be perfect in God's eyes.

19

Does Anyone Notice Me?

*Cleaning your house while your kids
are still growing is like shoveling the
walk before it stops snowing.*

PHYLLIS DILLER

It had been a busy week. While Art and the boys were gone on a mission trip to help the victims of a recent hurricane, the girls and I celebrated Thanksgiving with some friends. I had kept a great attitude about the whole thing. I was even surprised by how okay I was to be home with the girls alone during a major holiday. My daughters and I were having a great girls' weekend together when we suddenly got the hair-brained notion to completely decorate the house for Christmas and surprise the boys.

Now my husband is no Ebenezer Scrooge. He loves Christmas as much as I do. However, he does not love pulling out all of the decorations from the attic, assembling the tree, untangling and stringing the lights, and fussing with getting the decor just right. What a gift we could give him this year! What joy he could have if he walked in and all the work had been done. How happy he'd be if his only job setting up Christmas this year was to simply enjoy the beauty and compliment the decorators!

The girls and I kicked it into high gear. I enlisted the help of a sitter to supervise and assist the girls while I ran errands, bought a few things to spruce up some of our tired-looking decorations, purchased some gifts, and then bought the wrapping paper and gift tags to complete our mission. We assembled two trees, carefully placed the nativity set, hung greenery throughout the house, put wreaths in windows and on doors, wrapped presents, lit candles, and stood back to admire our great masterpiece.

We were so excited when we saw Art driving down the driveway. We were giddy with anticipation. He walked into the house and...it was business as usual. He kissed me, told the kids hello, and walked to the bedroom to put away his things. He mumbled something as he headed for the bedroom, but I didn't hear quite what he said. He may have commented that the house looked nice, but that was certainly NOT the showstopping exclamation I was expecting. I stood speechless at first. Then I got mad!

This had been a fabulous plan. However, it did have one little flaw. I had set the bar so high for how I expected my husband to react that no man could have possibly met my expectations. I was looking for him to gasp with sheer delight. I wanted Art to affirm me, make me feel important, and appreciate all that I do. I wanted to be noticed and hear the acclaim of his pleasure in my job well done. Now, none of these expectations would have been bad in and of themselves. (Well, except the gasp with sheer delight part.) I do want my husband to notice my efforts. But when he did not notice me, my reaction showed a heart problem. I felt more than slighted. I felt rejected on a very deep level. And it smacked me square in the face that my soul was depleted.

Had my soul been full of Jesus' love, acceptance, and His perspective-changing truths, my husband's response would not have sent me into a tailspin. I could have seen it for what it really was. My man is not wired to be awed by decor, plain and simple. So he didn't notice. I could have pointed out my hard work and taken whatever praise he knew to give. Instead, I blew the whole event out of proportion and made it into an issue of great definition. "He doesn't care about me. He doesn't love me. He doesn't notice all I do." On and on the voices of insecurity taunted.

This need to hear that I am loved and appreciated stems from my past. It stems from a little girl who twirled in front of her daddy. Around and around my little body went while my heart was crying out, "Daddy, do you notice me? Daddy, am I your precious daughter? Daddy, do you think I'm special and beautiful?" But, my daddy never spoke these words of love into my life, and my heart has tried to play catch up ever since. Looking for what was missing in my childhood in misplaced ways is something God has been dealing with in my heart. He asked me recently, "Lysa, are you tired of being the child of a broken parent? Because I want you to be a child of God."

In other words, I must let God fill me. I must let His approval fill up the desperation in my heart. I need to stop searching, stop questioning, stop the unrealistic expectations of others.

> When you aren't depending on your husband to fill you up, then he can make mistakes and you are still okay. He can say the wrong thing, and you can forgive him quickly. He can struggle and question his direction, and you don't fall into despair. He can be your partner and your friend, because he does not have to be your Savior. When you are living in the fullness of Christ, your children are being sloshed with His grace and tenderness…They can disappoint you and not bear the scars of your pride and your pain. They can grow up to be vibrant, independent-thinking, loving adults because they did not have to be your Savior.[1]

How do I transfer my identity from that of a child of a broken parent to that of being a child of God? I remind myself of some fundamental truths:

- My dad's issue of not being able to show me the love and affirmation I needed had nothing to do with me. He was broken from his own hard life experiences. I was not the broken one.

- Holding on to the hurt and constantly misplacing the desire to be affirmed will give me the opposite of what I desire. Instead of feeling fulfilled, I'll feel more and more needy as those closest to me pull away. For them, it is exhausting trying to meet someone's needs, only to be constantly told their efforts are not enough. For me, it is exhausting to try and prove I am worthy of someone's love, only to constantly feel I am not good enough.

- Writing down verses that affirm my identity as a child of God and meditating on them often will remind me of the truth—and the truth will always set me free (John 8:32).

- I need to make the choice to be a child of God, day by day, reaction by reaction, moment by moment. I need to consider the reality of the situation I'm in without letting misguided emotions cloud my outlook.

- Finally, when I feel those old insecure emotions start to creep back into my heart, I need to immediately give them to Jesus and ask Him to remove them and replace them with His truth.

I took all my hurt about my Christmas decorations not being noticed and mentally handed it to God. I closed my eyes and once again saw myself as a little girl twirling about. Around and around I saw my little body go, only this time a smile had replaced the look of desperate longing. For the audience was not a broken daddy or an unknowing husband, but rather a perfect and loving heavenly Father. He whispers to me, "I love you. I love how I made you. I notice all you do and I am pleased." And I whisper back, "I know. I finally know."

Refresh My Soul

Read Psalm 16:5; 73:26; 119:57.

Is God your portion today? "Because of the LORD's great love we are not consumed, for his compassions never fail. They are new every morning; great is your faithfulness. I say to myself, 'The LORD is my portion; therefore I will wait for him'" (Lamentations 3:22-24).

These verses speak of God's unfailing love for us (*hesed* in the Hebrew). This word *hesed* describes a love that is steadfast and loyal. God's love is not dependent on our deservedness. He loves us no matter what simply because we are His children.

In this chapter, I mentioned writing down verses that affirm that I am a child of God. I have listed some references for you to look up to make this easier for you to do right now. Spend some time writing down the ones that speak to your heart. Meditate on what it means to be God's child. Finish by writing a prayer of thanksgiving and praise for making you His child and for loving you exactly as you are.

Psalm 2:7

John 1:12-13

Acts 13:32-33

Romans 8:14-17

Galatians 4:4-7

Ephesians 5:1

2 Corinthians 6:18

Hebrews 2:10-12

1 John 3:1-2

20

When My Plans Fail

The roses under my window make no
reference to former roses or better ones;
they are what they are; they exist with
God today. There is no time to them.
There is simply the rose; it is perfect
in every moment of its existence.

RALPH WALDO EMERSON

I was so thrilled at the surprise trip I had planned for Brooke and Ashley. I was booked to speak at an event in Orlando, Florida. The coordinator of the event offered to get some free tickets to Disney World if I wanted to bring a couple of my kids with me. I decided not to keep it a surprise as I realized that half the fun of a trip like this is the anticipation of getting to go. So together we ticked off the months, weeks, and days until it was time.

The day before we were leaving, I dropped the kids off at school, worked out, showered, and dressed, and then headed to the office to tie up some last-minute details. On my way there I noticed my cell phone had two missed calls and two messages showing on the face screen. I dialed my voice mail and started listening to the messages. They were both from the same person and had the same frantic tone to them. It was the event planner in Orlando calling to tell me she was at the airport to pick me up but couldn't find me and the kids.

I didn't panic at first. I simply called my office and with a nervous chuckle told my assistant that this poor lady was so tired from planning the event that she must have gotten confused. To my horror she was not the one confused—I was! I should have flown out that morning and already been enjoying the rides at Disney with my girls. I whipped the car around, ran home to literally throw our clothes in a suitcase, and zipped to the school to pick up the girls. Then we were off to the airport, where I found out how expensive it can be to miss your flights and have to rebook three tickets. After we were finally settled on the plane, I closed my eyes. I was exhausted, frustrated, and quite embarrassed. I had such high hopes for this trip. I had been so excited about taking Ashley and Brooke to experience a day and a half at Disney World. Now we'd only have one half day. I lifted up my plans to the Lord and asked for His help.

Lord, You know I had good plans for me and my girls. But I have messed up, and now I am feeling very stressed that this whole trip might turn out in shambles. I didn't get to pack everything I wanted us to have. I didn't get to map out a plan for our time there. And now that our time will be cut so short, what's the use? Lord, will You restore our trip? Lord, will You arrange our minutes at Disney so that it will be full of fun and so that we each get to do our favorite things while there?

As soon as we landed I sensed God had already answered our prayers. The event coordinator met us at the airport with big gift bags full of supplies for our day at Disney. She had thought of everything from autograph books and rain ponchos to snacks and water bottles. When we checked into our hotel, we found out we'd been upgraded to a suite at no charge and they were throwing in a complimentary dinner. After dinner, we went to go see the concierge, and he told us how to maximize our short time there and gave great suggestions on where to be at certain times.

That night we took a boat ride, went on a horse-and-carriage tour, cooked s'mores at a campfire, and watched Disney movies under the stars in an outdoor theater. The next morning everything at the event I was speaking at went well. Ashley loved getting dressed up and eating the yummy brunch food, and Brooke even got up on stage and prayed for everyone. Then we were off to Disney. We got a map, sat down for a quick lunch, and made a list of our must-see attractions. We figured out the Fastpass options to avoid long lines and set out on our grand Disney adventure. Ashley wanted to ride the fast rides and Brooke was all about seeing the princesses. Though we only had five hours, I sensed God was redeeming our time.

The most special moment came in a very unexpected and unplanned way. We happened to be walking by the carousel and suddenly a man dressed in an elaborate Merlin costume stepped up on a nearby stage where a large crowd was forming. We joined the crowd in anticipation for a show he promised would be extra special. Merlin stood by a huge stone and asked for a volunteer from the audience to try and pull his sword from the stone. A large burly man was chosen, but despite his obvious strength and all his efforts, he could not pull the sword from the stone. So, Merlin got his special tuning fork out and scanned the crowd for just the right person. He went to the left. He went to the right. He scanned back and forth and suddenly landed on Brooke. Her eyes lit up as she was brought up front and instructed by Merlin on what to do. She was to pull the sword from the stone.

Her strength paled in comparison to the strong man. She was so short they had to get a step stool for her to stand on. The strong man had looked so qualified and so sure of himself as he stood before the stone. Brooke looked small, unsure, and, quite honestly, unable. But as she reached down and grabbed the large sword, the stone split apart and released Merlin's sword. Now, I understand that at Disney *magic* often happens with a little help from mechanical devices and secret switches, so I wasn't so amazed by the sword and stone trick as what happened afterward.

Merlin reached in his trunk and pulled out a queen's cape, tiara, gold medal, and certificate naming Brooke as "Queen of the Realm" for the day. It was by far the highlight of the day. She still has her certificate and medal, and she loves to remind us that she is official royalty.

As we boarded the plane that night to head home, I thanked God for redeeming our trip. Just when I thought I'd messed up everything, I asked for His help and He answered. This trip wound up being better than any of us ever imagined it would be.

Your motherhood adventure can be better than you ever imagined as well. Do you get discouraged when your plans aren't unfolding as you'd hoped? Maybe you planned a great day out at the park with the kids, and then on the way there you got stuck in traffic, you forgot half the picnic lunch on the counter at home, you locked your keys in the car, and little Suzie got stung by a bee. You feel your blood pressure escalating. Instead of this being the positive investment you intended it to be, you find yourself yelling at the kids and wishing you'd just stayed home.

Do you ever beat yourself up for things not being as organized as you wish they were? I've talked to a lot of moms who struggle with being discouraged over this issue. One mom said, "I just can't seem to get on top of things. I mean, I clean one room while the kids destroy another. I have grand plans to finally cook a meal that doesn't come out of a box, and no one likes it." Oh, honey, I understand your frustration.

For me, it's the scrapbooks that never get done, the lack of video footage, the constant hunt for misplaced items, and a filing system that leaves a lot to be desired. Maybe if my filing system were a little more organized, I wouldn't have missed my flight to Orlando! But the reality is, we all fall short and must rely on God. Becoming frustrated and mad will completely drain us and make us feel defeated. Turning our circumstances over to God will right our heart, change the way we look at the situation, and help us recognize glimpses of God in the midst of our broken efforts.

The Bible has a lot to say on this topic:

Many are the plans in a man's heart, but it is the LORD's purpose that prevails (Proverbs 19:21).

Commit to the LORD whatever you do, and your plans will succeed (Proverbs 16:3).

In his heart a man plans his course, but the LORD determines his steps (Proverbs 16:9).

Remember that everything that happens to you is first filtered through God's hand. Interruptions can become opportunities. What you might see as distractions God might see as divine appointments. Things may happen that seem so haphazard and distracting to our agenda, but with a fresh dose of perspective, they can turn into precious moments.

I think I'll go get Brooke's "Queen of the Realm" medal and put it on. I'll wear it while I brave the closet where my disorganized photos keep calling my name. Surely, God has a surprise for me in there. Maybe I'll even find the picture I took of my sweet little girl wearing the medal with the royal cape draped about her shoulders, holding her certificate, and smiling. I hope I always remember the day my plans completely failed but God made a way for my child to exclaim, "This was one of my best days ever!"

Refresh My Soul

Read Psalm 25:4-10; 32:8.

When your plans fail, what does that mean to you? Does it mean your plans were wrong? Does it mean that God did not bless your plans? Or does it mean that you simply needed to spend more time seeking God's face and determining *His* plans?

In both of these passages, the verses mention the words "teach" and "instruct." Do you have a teachable heart? What do you think it means to have a teachable heart?

Isaiah 28:26 says, "His God instructs him and teaches him the right way." As a mom, I often find myself in the role of teacher and instructor. Whether I am showing my kids how to tie their shoes or ride a bike, or helping them with homework, I love showing them how to do new things. I rejoice in their successes and try my best to guide them in the way that is right and best for them. However, my teaching and instruction can only work if they are willing to receive and take in what I have to share.

As our heavenly Father, God also wants to teach us and instruct us. He wants to see us succeed. God loves us enough to do whatever it takes to keep us on the right path—a path that leads to Him. Isaiah 2:3 says, "He will teach us his ways, so that we may walk in his paths."

Sometimes this requires His discipline. As moms, we know that to raise up a well-behaved child, we must discipline them sometimes. It is not the best part of our job, but it is no less necessary. In Deuteronomy 8:3, Moses tells the people: "[God] humbled you, causing you to hunger and then feeding you with manna, which neither you nor your fathers had known, to teach you that man does not live on bread alone but on every word that comes from the mouth of the LORD."

What does this verse tell you about where you can find God's instruction?

The Israelites received God's instruction through Moses. We receive God's instruction through His Word, the Bible. If we want to know how to make our plans succeed, we can go to His Word for answers. He is there for us the way we are there for our kids. His character is woven into every story, His wisdom etched in every line of the text. All we have to do is look.

Read Psalm 37:5-6.

In verse 5, the word "commit" means literally "to roll." We are to roll everything in our lives—the burdens and trials, the successes and failures—onto Him. He is capable of handling all of it. He *wants* to handle all of it if we will only pause long enough to hand it over instead of trying to carry it all ourselves. We can trade our burdens for crowns, pulling the sword from the stone with ease because we have the strength of the Lord behind us!

What do you need to commit to the Lord today? Are you seeking what He has to teach you through His Word?

21

Missing the Forest for the Trees

*The only measure of what you believe
is what you do. If you want to know
what people believe, don't read
what they write, don't ask what they
believe, just observe what they do.*

ASHLEY MONTAGU

Sometimes I'm guilty of being such a rule follower that I can't think outside the box. For example, I was cooking a meal recently while on the phone with a friend. I gasped as I realized I hadn't allowed enough time to cook a casserole before company was to arrive. My friend told me to turn up the oven temperature to allow the food to cook faster. That option had never occurred to me. Isn't it breaking some hard and fast cooking rule to cook a dish at a different temperature than what is specified on the recipe? Maybe for some things, but my simple casserole turned out fine.

This silly little experience opened my eyes to the fact that sometimes I look at things from too narrow a perspective. I can get so caught up in the rules that I miss the bigger picture. I was guilty of not seeing the forest for the trees, as the old saying goes. I prayed and asked God to get my attention the next time I looked at something too narrowly.

Well, get my attention He did! A few days later I assigned two things to my homeschooled children for their language arts lesson. First, they were to write a one-page paper about a place they wanted to visit and what they wanted to do once they got there. Second, they were to memorize a writing selection I'd picked from a book. As my kids turned in their papers, I was intrigued by the places they wanted to visit. One wanted to go to Miami to see famous basketball players. Another wanted to go to Hawaii. Yet another wanted to go to a made-up Candy Land town with her best friend. When Ashley, my nine-year-old middle daughter, turned in her paper, I was instantly frustrated because the city name was spelled incorrectly. I read through the rest of it and found many more grammatical errors and misspelled words.

I thought, *She doesn't think enough of this assignment to do her best work. Is she really struggling with spelling and grammar, or is this a heart issue? What does this say about her work ethic? What does this say about her character? What does this say about her educational future?*

I sent her to her room with instructions to write the paper over and do her best this time. I rushed back into my to-do list for the day and did not give the writing assignment another thought. That is, until I saw her original work tossed aside on the counter and read it one more time. Here is an excerpt written as it was on that paper:

Monrwia (Monrovia)

I want to go to Africa and see the litter (little) kids in the orfneg (orphanage). And brig (bring) them sutuff (stuff) like clous (clothes), toys, shous (shoes), blakits (blankets), and moms and dads. I want to pick up the litter (little) kids and hug them. Maybe I can be an ortnesig (orphanage) helper one day and make it a good place.

Talk about not seeing the forest for the trees. Had I really been reading the paper I could have celebrated the beauty in Ashley's heart. Instead, I was looking at the surface and catching every mistake I came across.

It's easy to slip into the mode of looking at but not really seeing our kids. Our hectic schedules leave little white space to venture beyond surface issues. Are their teeth brushed? How many servings of vegetables did they eat today? Did they make their bed? Did they dot their *i*'s and cross their *t*'s and use proper grammar? Did they score a goal? How many A's were on their last report card?

Yes, some of these things are important, but in light of eternity what really matters is their heart. Let me encourage you to learn from my mistake. Capture a moment today in which you really see someone else. Look beyond their surface mistakes to see their heart. Maybe it's your child. Maybe it's a spouse, neighbor, or friend.

About the second assignment I'd given that day, the memorization selection? Well, I think I'd do well to memorize it as well!

True worth is in being, not seeming;
In doing each day that goes by
Some little good; not in dreaming
Of great things to do by and by.
For whatever men say in this blindness,
In spite of the fancies of youth,
There's nothing so kingly as kindness,
And nothing so royal as truth.
Alice Cary

Refresh My Soul

Read Psalm 18:31-36.

Have you been striving for perfection and missing the mark? Has your quest for perfection led to disappointment? Have you put perfection ahead of relationships? How can you stop this from happening in your life?

Sure, we would all love to be perfect. We would love to have perfect kids, maintain a perfectly clean house, and cook perfectly delicious dinners. If we could attain perfection, then we would never have any more worries, right?

The truth is, that's not gonna happen this side of heaven. When Adam and Eve sinned, perfection left the Garden and sin entered in. Satan began his rule as the prince of this earth. He became Enemy Number One for those of us who call Jesus Lord of All.

Perfection, then, is just not possible here on earth. But we chase after it because it gives us something to strive for. Like a dog chasing its tail, it gives us a purpose, however misguided. Why did I want my kids' papers to be perfect? The truth is, because I knew that it would reflect well on me as their teacher. I cared little about the feelings the papers echoed, the pieces of their hearts I was given a glimpse of…until God got my attention.

Does He have your attention today?

Spend today focusing on your children's hearts. Just for today, don't focus on what they look like, act like, or talk like. Don't let Satan tempt you into misdirecting your attention towards superficial things. Dig past all the stuff on the outside, all the stuff screaming for your attention. Dig deep. Listen. Ask questions. Pray with them and hear their souls echoing in their prayers. Push out the busyness and sit.

Be still (Psalm 46:10).

Wait (Psalm 130:5).

Rest (Psalm 62:1).

When you do these things, you will find that perfection becomes much less important. Your priorities will fall into place because you will have connected with your kids. You might even see that some of the things you were worried about seem to fix themselves. Your insecure child might display some courage you didn't know she had in her. Your angry, sullen child might stop lashing out at others. Your kids will feel more secure when they know that you care about them and want to know them on a heart level.

Stop chasing perfection and let God make your way perfect, as the psalm says (Psalm 18:32). His definition of perfect will probably not look the way yours does. God cares about your heart and the hearts of your children. He understands that you can never be perfect and He loves you anyway. Spend some time today thanking Him for that truth.

22

Do They See Jesus in Me?

What I do know a lot about is why kids in Christian homes rebel. And although there are other reasons, one of the main reasons has to do with the way the average family goes about living the Christian life.

Dr. Tim Kimmel

O f all my childhood memories, there are a few I think of often and can recall in precise detail. I remember my stepdad bringing home a hand-me-down typewriter from his office. Though most people would have thought it to be trash, to me it was an absolute treasure. I placed my hands on the keys and wondered what it would take to unleash the hidden power of one's hands being able to fly into motion and type pages of legible words. I loved the rap-tip-tap sound the keys made as the letters struck the paper one by one. I envisioned myself finishing the final page of a book, swinging the carriage return lever across, hearing the bell ding, zipping the page free, and placing it on a neat stack of a manuscript beside me. My manuscript. I sighed. I didn't know enough words at that point to write an entire book, but one day I would. One day.

There was another time my parents had taken my sister and me to a meeting they had. We were instructed to go into the adjoining room and play with the other children. I'm not sure what triggered my desire to try and fulfill my lifelong dream of soaring through the air, but something must have. Maybe a dare from another kid or maybe too much soda, but whatever it was I soon found myself standing on top of a table announcing I could fly. Pointing to another nearby table, I prepared for my feat. I stretched my arms up like Superman, squished my face into a powerful-looking expression, lowered my head, and jumped. The kids all stood at attention ready to either witness an amazing miracle or a most gruesome injury from one foolish little girl. In midair I had great potential to be the hero of the meeting hall that night. But right before I reached the other table, my body flipped and I split open the back of my head. So close, yet so far.

But one of my favorite memories is one where I was sitting in a bay window in our den. My little fingers are ticking off the years until I would be a teenager, a college student, a wife, and a mommy. I remember being so sad at how long it would be until I could start my own family and have my own home. It seemed as though it would be forever before I was a grown-up. What a wonderful thing it would be to be a real grown-up. You can do what you want to do. Go where you want to go. Get together with your friends. And never have the stresses of life, such as bedtimes and report cards. If only I'd known! Now, I sit and think about how nice it would be to be a kid again. Can you count backward on your fingers?

Combine these images with my mom making my favorite gingersnap cookies, a birthday party where we rented a movie projector from the local library and watched the black-and-white version of *King Kong,* the girl who sat next to me in third grade and gave me head lice, and painting my bedroom bubble gum pink with a roller and walking around with pink splatter on me for days—and that is my childhood. Not every memory, but the ones that dance in the forefront of my mind.

It's amazing to me that a whole childhood of experiences can be condensed down to just a few paragraphs. You would think that the highlights of my childhood would have been a trip to Disney World, a Christmas morning when I got every gift on my list, or an elaborate costume made just for me. But my most vivid memories are just random snapshots of ordinary days.

My children are always fascinated when I share with them things I remember from my childhood. These memories are especially meaningful when I point out how these stories relate to my life now. The story about me getting that typewriter as a child was an excellent memory to point out that even back then, God was preparing me for my calling as an author. My desire to fly also had a hint of things to come. I was a risk taker back then and continue to be a risk taker for God today. Not that I have continued to physically defy gravity, but my walk with God has been characterized by leaps of faith.

It is not only fun to share these stories with my children, it's also important for their character development. My kids are wide-eyed with wonder as they listen to the stories, and later they can recall them in surprising detail. It's amazing how well they remember the life lesson that I tie to the story. I think that's why Jesus taught with stories. While it may be difficult for a child to recall a passage of Scripture they just read, most can specifically recall the details of a story.

So much about our life stories can be traced back to the hand of God working in our lives. My children must meet the reality of Jesus in my life if they are to really take hold of Him for *their* lives. In *Why Christian Kids Rebel,* Tim Kimmel explains the number one reason that children walk away from the faith is that they never see it make a real difference in the lives of their parents.

Unfortunately, we can experience a safe and successful Christian life without being passionate about the Lord. As Christians how do we measure success? In our westernized view, success is measured in ways that are easily quantifiable: how much do you know about God, how much you serve, what public policies you embrace, what kind of Christian friends you have, your spiritual reputation, the kind of money you make, the amount of money you give to God, how few hassles you have in life, how well your kids behave, and how consistent your spiritual routine is. The problem is that all these can be enjoyed without having to passionately walk with God. But our kids, especially our most honest ones, are looking for something more authentic. When it isn't there, it's easy for them to be drawn to other options that work against everything we've tried to teach them.[1]

Not only do I trace the hand of God in my past stories, but I constantly look for ways to exemplify Jesus today. I point out answers to things we've prayed about. I show them the many ways God provides and make sure they know where credit is due. I live my faith out loud and up front so they cannot miss that Christ is the center of our home. He has become too real to deny.

Where I am challenged is making sure my attitude doesn't discredit the reality of Christ. Again, not that I feel the pressure to be perfect—that would be unrealistic and fake. But I have to be on guard when I'm tired, drained, hormonal, or frustrated by some life circumstance. These are times I need to press in to God, ask for His strength, call on Him to fill my emotional gaps moment by moment, and go to bed early. It is so easy to slip into reacting in the flesh and leaving a wake of yuck behind me. But even when I fail with my attitude, I can see it as a chance to exemplify the reality of Jesus in how I handle my failure. If I am quick to humble myself, ask for forgiveness, and model redemption, that speaks volumes to my kids as well about how real Jesus is in my life.

What memories will my kids hang on to in their adulthood? What ordinary day will forever be burned in their instant recall? What words will they use to describe their childhood? I have no idea. I have hopes of how wonderfully they'll remember our home. I pray for the bad days to be erased and the great days to be magnified. But most of all I pray that it is the reality of Jesus that becomes the bedrock of their souls.

Refresh My Soul

Read Psalm 28:6-9.

Do you remember my story about trying to fly by leaping from a table?

These verses in Psalm 28 speak of a different kind of leaping—when your heart leaps within you for sheer joy. Have you ever had that happen? I have. When a handsome young man named Art asked me on a date for the first time, my heart leapt for joy within me. When I cradled my newborn baby, Brooke, and thought of Mary—who also welcomed a very special new baby—my heart leapt for joy within me. When our two boys spent their first night in our home as our adopted sons, my heart leapt for joy within me at the blessing of being able to tuck them into bed as their mom.

Think back over your life and pinpoint some specific moments that made your heart leap for joy. Allow your mind to wander down memory lane. Then write these moments down. If you are facing difficulties, it is helpful to remember these times and meditate on happy memories. If your memories involve your children, find a quiet moment to share these memories with them.

If your memories involve your husband, find a private moment to share them with him. (Don't assume he already knows!)

Think of a few of your childhood stories and life lessons you learned. Record one memory from childhood that you can see God's hand in.

Record a recent memory in which the reality of Jesus was evident in your life.

Spend some time in prayer, thanking and praising God for these moments in your life. Now, according to the verses that you read today, thank Him also for being:

your strength (verse 7)

your shield (verse 7)

a God you can put your trust in (verse 7)

your helper (verse 7)

your fortress (verse 8)

your salvation (verse 8)

your shepherd (verse 9)

the One who carries you (verse 9)

Reread verse 9. Read Isaiah 40:11.

In what areas of your life are you effectively modeling Jesus to your children? What areas do you need to work on? Write out a prayer of celebration and confession and ask God for His strength to make real changes in this area.

Being a mom is hard. It is hard to model the right attitudes for our children. It is hard to live out our convictions in front of our children and be like Christ. We know that our decisions, our words, and our actions all shape who our children become. Talk about pressure! I am thankful we don't have to do motherhood alone. I praise Jesus that He serves as our shepherd, gently leading those of us who are trying to lead these little people. Copy Isaiah 40:11 and post it somewhere you can see it throughout your day. When you feel overwhelmed by the formidable job of motherhood, claim this verse and call on Jesus to help you. And be sure to give Him your praise.

"I will extol the LORD at all times; his praise will always be on my lips. My soul will boast in the LORD; let the afflicted hear and rejoice. Glorify the LORD with me; let us exalt His name together" (Psalm 34:1-3).

23

Chasing Rainbows

That it will never come again is
what makes life so sweet.

EMILY DICKINSON

I think often about being an older woman and reflecting back on this time of my life. I know this will happen because I already catch myself pondering backward. Thoughts of yesterday tumbling into today are mixed with sighs and smiles. How quickly the years go by, and almost without warning we enter into new phases and stages. How unaware we live. I can't remember the day that marked the last diaper changed, the last bottle fixed, the last time I would kiss my baby's chubby cheek and see them run to me with up-stretched arms babbling, "Hold you me. Hold you me, Mommy." Yet there was a day that proclaimed, "This is the last time for this task that seems so mundane today but precious and priceless tomorrow." Those benchmark days come and go as all days have a habit of doing.

So I want to think now of what I might think then. For now I have the opportunity to make changes and adjustments to live a life of no regrets. Just recently I heard of a mom who signs her letters and e-mails with "striving to be an old woman with no regrets." That's how I want to sign off on the pages of my life—that I loved and laughed and lived with no regrets.

I don't want to be the older woman sitting at the park watching other people live and love and laugh and think about all the simple pleasures I missed out on with my children. Why didn't I sit in the backyard and blow bubbles? Why didn't we lie in the grass and name the shapes of the clouds above us? Why didn't we read a fairy tale and then find a toad and kiss him just to see? Why didn't we talk longer, play harder, and spend more time dreaming together? And did we even once chase a rainbow's end?

This point was made so clear to me as my kids and I ran errands one day. Some days I see errands with the kids as opportunities for great learning experiences. Making a bank deposit, getting a document notarized, shopping for good deals at the secondhand store, and changing the oil in the car are skills my children will one day require. Other days, to be honest, I see having the children along as a pain. There is nothing worse than being trapped in the confined space of a vehicle with bad attitudes and whiney voices. But even these moments can be great character-shaping times, as long as Mom can keep her cool.

It was an errand day when one of my daughters spotted a rainbow. I quickly called my friend Marybeth to tell her of our discovery so she might usher her kids outside in hopes of seeing the colorful display. She commented, "This is the beauty of motherhood. You get to experience and appreciate childhood things like rainbows with your kids." Her thought impacted me in a deep and wondrous way. It became a mental snapshot—a moment frozen in time—this amazing rainbow-chasing moment that will bring a smile to my face when it is wrinkled and pondering.

The rainbow was amazing. Its red, orange, yellow, green, blue, indigo, and violet colors splashed across the sky in a grand and glorious fashion. It looked as though it could be a permanent fixture, reminding me of the story of Noah and God's promise to never again flood the earth. But I hardly got to the thought of the animals coming to the ark two by two before the colors started to swirl and fade. Almost as quickly as the rainbow burst onto the scene of our ordinary day, its extraordinary beauty peaked and then dissipated. As we drove down our driveway, we watched the last of the colors disappear into the clouds. Though I was sad to see God's artwork taken off display, I rejoiced that my kids and I had taken the time to chase the rainbow's end.

Our children are like that rainbow. They burst on the scene of our lives in such a way that you feel as though they'll be there forever. Their colorful personalities and bright expressions are shining reminders of God's promises and miracles. They dance through their childhood, making lasting impressions on our hearts, and then the time comes for them to pull away. The colors of childhood swirl and mix and change and fade into the realities of adulthood. It will happen. There will come a day when the door to childhood will open for the last time, and that night, as surely as that child closes her eyes to sleep, the door will close. All the curious questions that drive you crazy today will cease. All the fingerprints and smudges will go away. All the childhood fantasies and dreams will fade. And her mother will wake the next morning to peer into the sky and wonder where the rainbow has gone.

Intentionally letting go of mommy stress and choosing to enjoy motherhood enables us to capture these times. I want to become a family that lives better, richer lives. I want to know my children at a deeper level than the hustle and bustle of a stressed-out life allows. To know my children on a deeper soul level is to come to discover the joy of parenting.

The real joy of parenting will be watching this child God has entrusted into my care grow to be a healthy, capable adult. Mixed with the sadness of seeing the doors of childhood close is a great sense of accomplishment.

I always thought an indicator of having raised a child well was when that child chose to become a doctor or a banker. But as I have come to really know my children and prayed about the stress inherent in a myriad of educational opportunities, I realize their potential is God given and therefore should be God directed and parent nurtured. In *The Art of Sensitive Parenting,* Katharine C. Kersey wrote, "Children come into the world not knowing who they are. They learn who they are from those around them."[1] I want my presence in my children's lives to nurture a confidence in God's plan for them, not just my plans or even their plans.

God has a purpose and a plan for each child. Jeremiah 29:11 assures us that God has plans to prosper and not harm us. So why do we fret so much more about educational benchmarks and test scores than the true measure of God's standards? In Deuteronomy 28 we are told about the blessings that will come for being obedient to God. "If you fully obey the LORD your God and carefully follow all his commands I give you today, the LORD your God will set you high above all the nations on earth. All these blessings will come upon you and accompany you if you obey the LORD your God: You will be blessed in the city and blessed in the country" (verses 1-3). Verse 12 goes on to say, "The LORD will open the heavens, the storehouse of his bounty, to send rain on your land in season and to bless all the work of your hands." He then concludes this powerful section by stating, "Do not turn aside from any of the commands I give you today, to the right or to the left, following other gods and serving them" (verse 14).

It is quite sobering then to go on and read the rest of this chapter, where God warns what will happen if we ignore His decrees and fall into disobedience. Deuteronomy 28:15-16 says, "However, if you do not obey the LORD your God and do not carefully follow all his commands and decrees I am giving you today, all these curses will come upon you and overtake you: You will be cursed in the city and cursed in the country." Verse 20 continues, "The LORD will send on you curses, confusion and rebuke in everything you put your hand to, until you are destroyed and come to sudden ruin because of the evil you have done in forsaking him."

Now let me state clearly, I am not legalistic and daily rejoice in the gift of God's grace. I also recognize that this was old covenant theology and we live under the new covenant of Jesus Christ. However, it is there. God did not have the Old Testament disappear when the Jesus rose from the dead and a new covenant was made. The theme of obeying God runs from Genesis to Revelation and is vital to our children's success in life. A child who has a heart that is willing to surrender to God and fulfill every divine appointment given to him or her is a success. That should be our benchmark. That should be our standard.

Yes, I want my children to have the very best opportunities available. Yes, I want them to learn in an environment of discovery and wonder. Yes, I want them to earn a college degree if their vocational choice demands that. But at the heart of it all we must take our noses out of textbooks and delve into *the* Book to gain God's perspective of raising and educating a child. We must become more concerned with their souls than their brains. A child's smarts can help them go places in life, but the character reflected from their soul is what will determine whether or not they do anything significant once they get there.

Chase those rainbows, my friend. Live a life of no regrets, and in the process teach your children how to run hard after God.

Refresh My Soul

Read Psalm 39:4-6; 89:47-48; 144:3-4.

Our time on earth truly is fleeting. The years whiz by almost in a blur, and we often shake our heads wondering where the time went. We have but a moment with our precious children. How will you spend that time?

It is so easy to get bogged down in the busyness of life, or as Charles Hummel so memorably put it—the tyranny of the urgent. We rush from one activity to the next, one spill to the next. One more fire to put out, one more check mark on our to-do lists. Do we notice the little people milling around us? Do we stop, get down on eye level with them, and let the world and all its demands fade into the background? Today, this day, will certainly pass us by, and tomorrow and the next day too. How are we spending our precious time with our children?

Read Mark 9:36-37; 10:13-16.

Jesus was busy. He was in demand. Wherever He went, a crowd followed. Each person in that crowd wanted a piece of Him. Ever feel like that? When little children approached, the disciples shooed them away. In the disciples' limited understanding, they thought that surely Jesus didn't have time to fool with little kids! But Jesus rebuked them. He knew that children are important in God's eyes. Is God stretching your character and broadening your world through the daily tasks of being a mom?

*Read Isaiah 11:6; Matthew 11:25-26; 18:1-6;
1 Corinthians 1:26-29.*

Can you think of something you have learned through one of your children recently? Maybe it is just how precious life is. Maybe it is how fast time flies. Write about what your kids are teaching you.

Spend some time in prayer evaluating your relationship with your kids. Do you know them? Do you know their hearts? Do you have time to spend just listening to them? If not, ask God to help you make time. I always say that T-I-M-E stands for "Take Initiative for Meaningful Experiences." How are you spending your time?

You may have developed bad habits of dismissing or disregarding your kids. You may have fallen victim to the world's attitude of children being a nuisance. May I challenge you today to see your children from God's perspective? I guarantee you will be blessed when you do!

"Then our sons in their youth will be like well-nurtured plants, and our daughters will be like pillars carved to adorn a palace… Blessed are the people of whom this is true; blessed are the people whose God is the LORD" (Psalm 144:12,15).

24

Remember to Look Up

*Keep your face to the sunshine, and
you cannot see the shadows.*

HELEN KELLER

Some people might think that what I do is glamorous. Flying to cities all over the country, speaking in front of thousands, and signing the books I've written sounds exciting, but it's really not. Let me paint a truer picture of the life of a Christian speaker and writer.

When everybody else is looking forward to a fun weekend of sleeping in, going to movies, and hanging out with their families, I am preparing to head off to do ministry. A couple weekends a month, I pack my bags, drive myself to the airport, park in a remote parking lot, catch the shuttle bus, lug my luggage all the way to the terminal, wait in long security lines (where I have to take off my shoes, jewelry, jacket, and belt, and then redress), rush to find my gate, and hopefully make my flight. Once I arrive at the event, I love what I do. Getting to minister to women is incredibly rewarding and encouraging, but it is a short part of the whole adventure.

I love writing books, but that is a lonely process as well. Imagine spending hours sitting in a quiet room surrounded by research papers, computer equipment, and notes that will help you turn out a book. A typical book contains more than 50,000 words. That's a lot of words, and it takes a lot of time thinking up and typing those words. Then there are the edits and the rewrites and wondering if it ever really will come together...

Now please don't misunderstand me. I am very grateful for the opportunity to be used by God in others' lives. There is such joy in leading women closer to the Lord. But I have to make the choice to see the joy and not get bogged down in the mundane duties that surround the calling.

Motherhood is a lot like that.

It sounds so dreamlike to dress your little darlings in clothes that match, hear them say that you are the best mom in the world, bake cookies together in the afternoon, and relish their sweet spirits while listening to their bedtime prayers. Yes, those moments are there. But woven all around ideal moments are whiney voices, childish attitudes, sibling fights, strong wills, messy accidents, snotty noses, stained clothes, and strained nerves. It all comes down to choosing what to focus on. Wherever you put your focus, that will become bigger and more magnified.

In the book of Philippians, God clearly explains what we are to focus on.

> Finally, brothers, whatever is true, whatever is noble, whatever is right, whatever is pure, whatever is lovely, whatever is admirable—if anything is excellent or praiseworthy—think about such things. Whatever you have learned or received or heard from me, or seen in me—put it into practice. And the God of peace will be with you (Philippians 4:8-9).

"It is not enough to hear or read the Word of God, or even know it well. We must also put it into practice. How easy it is to listen to a sermon and forget what the preacher said. How easy it is to read the Bible and not think about how to live differently.

How easy it is to debate what a passage means and not live out that meaning. Exposure to God's Word is not enough. It must lead to obedience."[1]

For us moms, let's take a look at each section of this verse and bring it home in everyday terms.

Whatever is true. It is a blessing to be a mom. There are thousands of women with empty arms that would trade places with us in a heartbeat. Motherhood has its hard days and hard seasons, but they don't have to be our focus and they won't last the whole journey long. God will fill in our gaps as we walk in obedience with Him. Think on such things.

Whatever is noble. The word "noble" is defined as "having or showing qualities of high moral character, such as courage, generosity, or honor." A noble mom is one who recognizes that children are taught most effectively by example. While kids remember what you say for the moment, they remember what they see lived out for a lifetime. Think on such things.

Whatever is right. A Christian's pursuit is to exemplify the righteousness of Christ in his or her life. But righteousness is a complicated word that can seem too big for everyday life. So I choose to look at righteousness as "making right choices that honor God daily." Look at each choice as one more step pointing you to a destination. If we want to leave a good legacy, we must make choices today that reflect that. Think on such things.

Whatever is pure. Matthew 5:8 says, "Blessed are the pure in heart, for they will see God." If I want to see God in my home, I must seek to purify my heart. If I want to see God in my marriage, I must seek to purify my heart. If I want to see God in my children's lives, I must seek to purify my heart. If I want to see God in my everyday life, I must seek to purify my heart. This doesn't mean I have to seek to be perfect. It means I must perfectly surrender my heart, my motives, my actions, and my reactions to Christ. Think on such things.

Whatever is lovely. Do I have a lovely view of motherhood? If someone were to ask me about being a mom, what would my first response be? What is the look that would immediately sweep across my face? When I examine my facial expressions, do they most often look lovely? Do I most often wear a smile and a pleasant expression, or do I most often wear a scowl and a frown? What would my kids say is my view of motherhood? Think on such things.

Whatever is admirable. The investment of time and energy you are putting forth in being a mom is admirable. The sacrifices you make both big and small are admirable. Your love for your children is admirable. The way you nurture, protect, and care for their needs is admirable. While the world may not esteem you, and while your kids may not rise up to call you blessed today, God notices. God sees all you do. God sees all you give. God says you are admirable and worthy of praise! Think on such things.

If anything is excellent or praiseworthy. The calling of being a mom is reason for great celebration and joyous praise to the Lord. You are participating in shaping a life for eternity. No matter how you have approached motherhood, up to this point you can choose to pursue excellence from this day forward. Praise God for second chances and that His mercies are new every morning! Think on such things.

I was thinking on such things on a recent flight from Illinois to Missouri. The day in Illinois had been very gray, dreary, and frightfully cold. It seemed as though the sun had taken a vacation and headed south. However, as we ascended from the ground and the plane broke through the clouds, I was astounded by the brightness of the sun. The sun had not gone anywhere. It was bright and warm and gleaming for miles.

That's when it hit me. The people below couldn't see the sun that day. If I had stayed on the ground, I might have been tempted to forget that it is always there. I might have focused on the gloomy, chilly clouds and allowed them to become bigger, more magnified, and the defining factor in my day. If I had stayed on the ground, I would not have the same perspective I had in rising above the clouds and seeing that the sun was still there. It was still bright and warm.

My heart filled with joy and a smile crossed my face as I turned my face and let the sunlight spill over it. It became bigger, more magnified, and redefined my day.

Lord, thank You for this visual reminder that even when the clouds of circumstance roll over my life and attempt to block my vision of You, You are still there. You are bigger than any circumstance. Your love, grace, forgiveness, and encouragement are there, even if I don't see them or feel them. You are bright and warm. Thank You for the days that I see You clearly. But even on the days that I don't, I will thank You still. For I know no matter how drained I feel, You are there. I know no matter how lonely I feel, You are there. I know no matter how overwhelmed I feel, You are there. I know through all my successes and failures as a mom, You are there. I just have to turn my face and my heart to You. When I focus on You, Jesus, You become bigger and more magnified than any problem I might be facing that day. You alone can redefine my day.

As I got off the plane in Missouri, I looked up to the sky. It was gray, cloudy, and very cold. Though no weather reports said it was a sunny day, I knew the truth. The sun was there. May the sun forever shine brightly on your face, and may the Son forever shine clearly in your heart. Remember to look up and let God redefine your days.

Refresh My Soul

Read Psalm 68:4; 123:1-2.

We worship the God of heaven. He sits on His throne on high. His hands will provide all our needs. His eyes are upon us.

For the eyes of the LORD range throughout the earth to strengthen those whose hearts are fully committed to him (2 Chronicles 16:9).

The eyes of the LORD are everywhere, keeping watch on the wicked and the good (Proverbs 15:3).

For the eyes of the Lord are on the righteous and his ears are attentive to their prayer (1 Peter 3:12).

Read Job 36:7; Jeremiah 24:6.

God is watching over you. He is watching over your children and your husband. Nothing happens on this earth that He does not see. We can rest in that fact and we can go to Him with the knowledge that He is aware of all that we face. He is not a disconnected, unfeeling God. He is part of our daily lives.

What is your response to His involvement in your life? If He is watching you, then where should your eyes be?

Read Psalm 25:15; 141:8; 2 Corinthians 4:18; Hebrews 12:2.

What are your eyes fixed on? Are they fixed on heaven or the things of this earth? Are you looking up to the Lord or all around you?

Think about your days. Evaluate your activities and where your eyes must be at all times. Your eyes must be on the condition of your home. Your eyes must be on the road as you drive. Your eyes must be on the safety of your children. Your eyes must be on the provisions your family needs. While your physical eyes must be on these things, where are your spiritual eyes?

"Turn my eyes away from worthless things" (Psalm 119:37). What worthless things are your eyes straying to? The pursuit of money and possessions? The attitudes and actions of those around you? Anxieties and concerns that should be handed over to God? Write down specific issues that your eyes are on in your life right now.

"Open my eyes that I may see wonderful things in your law" (Psalm 119:8). Make this your prayer today. Ask God to open your eyes that you may see only what He wants you to see.

Write down a prayer confessing the things that distract your eyes from Him and asking Him to reveal to you where and how to focus your eyes each day.

Write down Ephesians 1:18.

The eyes of your heart are your spiritual eyes. You can keep the eyes of your heart focused on God even when your physical eyes seem to be looking in 20 different directions. God knows your limits, He knows your desires, and He knows your heart. Trust Him as you focus the eyes of your heart in His direction.

Conclusion

The Choice Is Yours

I pray that you have laughed, cried, and enjoyed your journey through this book. I hope you feel inspired and encouraged to rediscover the joys of motherhood and that your motherhood experience will be different because of it. But this hope will not come about just because you've read the book. You have to make the choice to let it change things about your life. Rest assured, you are not alone. I made the choice to let this book change things about my life as I wrote it. May it be so for you as well.

Let's look back on this time together as a retreat of sorts. A short time where we did life together and God really spoke to our hearts. One of my favorite things to do as I end any retreat with women is to have a question and answer session with the attendees. Since that's really not possible for our situation, I thought I'd let you listen in on what a typical Q&A might be like by reading some of the questions I've been asked and answers I've given.

How did you meet your husband?

A guy friend of mine, Dean, called to tell me he played golf that day with the man I was going to marry. He also told me this guy was very nice, just my type, and would be at our group Bible study that next Wednesday. You'd better believe I put on my best outfit and made it to Bible study right on time!

As soon as I saw Art, I hoped Dean was right. He was the most handsome man I'd ever seen. It was love at first sight, only I didn't know he felt the same way. I knew he loved me the day he opened his restaurant just for me, on a day they are normally closed, and fixed me my favorite lunch.

How do you handle your children when they are disrespectful?

It is a privilege living in the TerKeurst family. If any of our children acts in a way that seems as though they are forgetting that privilege, we remind them. I tell my children that I am not their buddy or their slave. I am their mother, and I expect to be treated as such. We require our children to say "yes, ma'am," and "yes, sir." It is a Southern tradition that provides my kids the habit of practicing respect.

We expect our kids to obey quickly, quietly, and with a good attitude. We let them know that anything else will not be tolerated. They know the consequences of disobedience. Often we give them a choice between two consequences, such as lost privileges or extra chores.

Because I am highly allergic to rude children, we also expect our kids to have good manners. Two of my favorite things we've taught our kids is how we want them to answer the phone and how to properly introduce themselves. When answering the phone, we require them to say, "TerKeurst residence. This is (insert child's name here). May I help you?" Once they know whom the call is for, they hand the phone to the requested person quietly.

When introducing themselves to others, we have taught them to look the person in the eyes, give a firm handshake, and say, "Hi, my name is (child's name) TerKeurst. It is very nice to meet you."

What is something you feel all moms should know?

Our goal should not be to raise children; it should be to raise God-loving adults. I think in order to do this, reality discipline is a must. We must teach our children that there are consequences for making poor choices and irresponsible behavior. Let me assure you, I extend grace to my kids because I recognize that I so desperately need it myself. But I'm careful to balance grace with reality discipline. If you break something, I will forgive you, but chances are you'll have to pay to have it repaired or replaced. If you forget your lunch at home, I'll bring it to you once during the school year. After that, you'll have to get creative, and I bet you won't forget it again. If you forget to study for a test, I'll pray God gives you supernatural wisdom, but I will not write a note or let you miss school. These are all examples of reality discipline. The best thing about it is that it allows me to transfer the stress of poor choices back to the one who made that choice. It's very freeing for the mom and very memorable for the child.

How do you plan meals for so many people each week?

Please read the addendum at the end of this book called "Making Dinner Is Making Me Crazy." I give step-by-step instructions on how to participate in a cooking co-op, which has really been a life saver for me. Here is my schedule for the week:

Monday:

I cook for the cooking co-op.

Tuesday:

Dinner is delivered by a cooking co-op member.

Wednesday:

Quick dinner night. We either grab dinner at church or I cook something easy, such as tacos.

Thursday:

Dinner is delivered by a cooking co-op member.

Friday:

Pizza night

Saturday:

Leftovers night

Sunday:

Kids eat kid food and Mom and Dad go out for a date!

Is it hard to have a speaking ministry that requires travel with kids at home?

One of the best things I did when starting my ministry was getting my family involved. They know that this ministry thing is a family deal. I might be the mouthpiece, but each of them plays a vital role and receives blessings from God as a result. For example, Brooke is my prayer warrior. She always prays at home when she knows I am doing a session with an invitation to accept Christ. Since she has been doing this, the number of women who have accepted Christ at my conferences and retreats has tripled!

What are some common struggles you see moms all over the country having?

In today's high-stress, performance-driven society, I think a lot of moms are struggling to keep up. We constantly are grabbing for a measuring stick of sorts to see if we are successful moms and if our kids are excelling as much or more than everyone else. I don't want to get caught in the comparison trap. I want to point my kids to Jesus, tell them that He has a great plan for each of their lives, and instill in them the character to match their calling.

Of course, I do constantly wonder whether I am doing the best I can to teach them how to make the right choices in life. Will they take with them the lessons I've taught them? Are they prepared to make the right choices when I'm no longer there to help them through the consequences of those choices? The choices and consequences are small now, but when our children get older, these choices can be life changing.

A friend of mine, Michelle, was dealing with these same questions for her children and created a wonderful way to help her family learn about choices and the many consequences of them. Her motto is *"If you want to get really good at something, you have to practice, right? Now is the time to practice to help our children make good choices. This is too important to leave up to chance."*

What I love about Michelle's approach is that she is determined not to just celebrate her kids' achievements; she celebrates their good character. When her children make positive choices, she recognizes those choices. Knowing that character and values are the root of how we make decisions, she began focusing on the character traits that lead to those choices.

For example, when her four-year-old daughter, Emily, learned to ride her bike, her dinner was presented to her that evening on the family honor plate, a plate that only those who have shown good character and values receive the honor of dining on. When presented, her daughter knew why she was getting it and was very proud. She exclaimed that she was getting the honor plate because she learned to ride her bike today. She was kindly told NO. What? Yes, it was exciting that she learned to ride her bike today, but what filled Mommy and Daddy up with so much pride was her amazing attitude and the way she never gave up.

Every time she fell that day she got right back up and tried again. Four hours and an exhausted mom later, Emily was riding her bike. She had shown such perseverance that day that even if she hadn't learned to ride her bike, she still would have received the honor plate.

Emily made some big choices in how she chose to deal with the frustration of falling off her bike, missing the pedals, etc. She chose to turn her frustration into determination. She had the spotlight at dinner and was motivated to make the same choice in behavior when the opportunity presented itself again.

How do you have a quiet time with your busy life?

Sometimes I sit down and have an extended time of prayer and reading the Bible. Most times I only have time in the morning for a short devotion and prayer. (A great one I recommend is the free Proverbs 31 daily e-mail devotion. Go to www.Proverbs31. org to sign up.)

My time with the Lord is not something on my to-do list that I check off and forget about. I live a daily adventure with God. I am always talking to Him and constantly looking to His truths for direction. I don't have a stale religion where I go through the motions. I have a love relationship with God where I know He is with me all day, every day.

It grieves me when I hear women say that they can't wait for their kids to grow up so they can have "real quiet times." Satan loves to sell the lie to women that if we don't have hours to spend on our knees, then we shouldn't pray at all. If you have five minutes, then give that five minutes to God. If you have 30 minutes, then give that to God.

How do you stay rejuvenated?

I laugh a lot. I don't take myself too seriously. And I always look for God's hand in every situation. I'm also very intentional with planning fun things for myself.

Sometimes these fun things involve my husband and kids, other times they involve my friends, and sometimes it is just me and Jesus. On a spiritual level, I love to take a Bible verse and break it apart to unearth every hidden treasure contained within. I love to read inspirational Christian books that challenge me to think on deeper levels. I also love to go to bookstores, get a cup of my favorite coffee, and walk the aisles looking at all different kinds of books. I enjoy good girl movies that make me laugh, cry, and run home to kiss my husband! The silliest thing I do to get rejuvenated is go to the office supply aisle at Wal-Mart and buy something. I'm convinced I will have a whole room full of office supplies in my heavenly home. It will contain stick-it notes, my favorite medium-tip gel pens, paper clips of all shapes and sizes, and files that magnetically draw all the right papers inside of themselves. There will be no piles in heaven! That thought alone rejuvenates me.

Refresh My Soul

Read Psalm 33:12-15.

Just as we must make choices each day, so God has made a choice—the choice to welcome us into His kingdom if we will only accept Him. This passage shows us that God watches over us. He formed our hearts and knows us intimately. He knows the dark places, the things we don't tell anyone else. And He chose us anyway. What an awesome revelation!

Read 1 Samuel 16:7; Psalm 44:21; 139:23-24; Jeremiah 32:19.

These verses show that God knows our hearts. As our Creator, He fashioned us just the way He wanted us.

How does this knowledge make you feel? Are there parts of your heart that you hide from others? Have you ever thought about God seeing those parts and loving you anyway?

Read John 15:14-17; 2 Thessalonians 2:13-15.

Did you read these phrases? "You did not choose me, but I chose you" (John 15:16) and "From the beginning God chose you to be saved through the sanctifying work of the Spirit and through belief in the truth" (2 Thessalonians 2:13).

Spend some time today thinking about being chosen and how you can respond to that. Should this affect your attitude about life? Does it free you to know that God chose you in spite of all your flaws? Write your thoughts about this here or in your journal.

Your response to God is also a choice. Read the following verses and write down what choice you are asked to make based on each section of Scripture:

Deuteronomy 30:19-20

Joshua 24:15

Proverbs 8:10-11

Proverbs 16:16

Luke 10:41-42

John 7:17

We can choose to respond to God or pretend we never heard the truth. We can choose to live life differently from the world. We can choose to be a light to others through our attitude and actions. We can choose to reflect God to our children, to our spouse, and to everyone we encounter.

The passage in Joshua says to "choose for yourselves this day." You must choose each day to serve Him. You cannot choose just once for all time. You must renew your choice each day before the Lord. Before you put your feet on the floor each morning, you will make a choice that will carry you through that day.

The passage in Deuteronomy speaks of choosing blessing or cursing. Which will you choose? You can choose to bless or curse those you love with your words and your attitude. Is your motherhood experience based on a foundation that will not stand? Second Timothy 2:19 says, "Nevertheless, God's solid foundation stands firm, sealed with this inscription: 'The Lord knows who are His.'"

You are His child. He has chosen you and He loves you. Stand on His firm foundation and experience the blessings that will follow.

Addendum

Making Dinner Is Making Me Crazy

When it comes to cooking, five years ago I felt guilty "just adding water." Now I want to bang the tube against the countertop and have a five-course meal pop out. If it comes with plastic silverware and a plate that self-destructs, all the better.

ERMA BOMBECK

It had been one of those days. We've all had them. Suffice it to say, dinner was going to have to be a quick collection of random pantry items topped with stale crackers and lots of cheese. I whispered a little praise as I tucked my invention into the oven, "Thank You, God, for making cheese...it makes everything kid friendly and edible!"

Thirty minutes at 350 degrees, some boil-in-the-bag rice, a few rolls found in the depths of my freezer and voilà, dinner was served. Not a meal that would ever grace the cover of a gourmet cooking magazine, but a hot meal nonetheless. I had hardly put everything on the table when the questioning and complaining started.

"What is this?"

"Did you top it with those stale crackers from the pantry?"

"Why is there so much cheese?"

"I don't think I'm going to like this. Can I just have cereal?"

"Yeah, me too. Can I have cereal too?"

With each question I could feel my pulse quicken and the hair on the back of my neck starting to stand at attention. I shot back a mathematically sound answer, one that would surely make them immediately repent and see the error of their ways. "Do you know how many dinners I have to prepare for you in your lifetime? Do you? Try 7 nights x 52 weeks x 18 years, which equals a whopping 6552 meals!"

"Mom, I'm not trying to be mean or anything..."

I halted this child's misguided explanation with an age-old, tried-and-true motherly saying: "There are starving children in Africa who would give anything to have this meal!" I quickly realized this probably was not the best example to use, as we had adopted two of our kids from Africa. In a flustered attempt to quickly change my slip of the tongue, I added, "You used to be starving children in Africa. How can you turn up your nose at my dinner?"

I threw my hands in the air and fled to my bedroom. Making dinner, night after night, was making me crazy! I later recounted the evening's events to a friend, who told me she might have just the solution I was looking for, a dinner co-op. I would be responsible for making dinner for my family and two other families on Monday nights. Then I would have dinner delivered to me on Tuesdays and Thursdays. What a great idea!

I have been participating in the co-op for more than a year now and I love it. I asked the friend who first introduced this wonderful idea to me, Denise Covert, to jot down all the ins and outs to share with you. If making dinner is making you crazy, try this. It just might save your sanity too.

Cooking Co-op How-Tos:

Purpose:

- The purpose of the cooking co-op is to save time in preparation of dinners each week.

Benefits:

- More variety of meals (not all casseroles)
- Decreased monthly grocery cost

How It Works:

The following are basic guidelines that evolved from the principle that the co-op should make life easier. Each co-op will adapt and add to them over time.

- Groups of three families form a co-op. It works best with like-size or near like-size families.

- Each family provides one meal a week to the other two families, and in turn receives meals on designated nights.

- Each meal consists of one entree and two side dishes (dessert is not considered a side, but is always welcomed as an "extra").

- Examples: Lasagna, French bread, and salad; London broil, rebaked potatoes, and a can of green beans.

- The co-op is not intended to be a gourmet club. While gourmet dishes are welcome, food that is simple to prepare, for both the giver and receiver, is the order of the day.

- What you make is what you send...if you try something new and it doesn't come out the way you expected (that is, it looks funny, the portions too small, etc.), send it. You gave it an honest effort, and the idea is for this to be easy, not for someone to cook twice for the same meal.

- Each family purchases the following dishes:

  11x13 Pyrex baking dish
  8x8 Pyrex baking dish
  2.4 quart Tupperware (square container)

- The co-op cooks meet quarterly to plan menus. (We met every six weeks to start, but then as everyone got comfortable, we moved to every three months.) Bring entree ideas and calendars to each meeting, as well as comments regarding past meals.

- At the initial meeting, the cooks list likes, dislikes, and the cooking preferences of their family (examples: don't like peas, interested in low-fat meals, tend to cook spicy, etc.).

- A weekly schedule is worked out (example: the Browns are responsible for Monday night's meal, the Smiths are responsible for Tuesday night's meal, and the Joneses are responsible for Thursday night's meal).

- At this meeting, Jane Brown would take home two sets of the dishes and Mary Smith would take home one. This begins the rotation of dishes that assures you always have dishes available for the two other families when it's your time to cook.

- At this meeting, you plan a list of entrees for the next block of time. (This planning assures that you don't end up with filet mignon three nights in a row, but it need not be rigidly followed. If you planned on sending pork chops one night but had a lot of leftover ham from a party, you can switch.)

- You also determine delivery plans. The person who prepares the meal is responsible for delivery of the meal. (Again, how this works is individualized by the group—some groups would deliver it hot at mealtime, most would have it oven or stove ready. A set drop-off time can be arranged, a call before delivery can be made, or a key to each other's house can be exchanged.)

- When you deliver the meal, you also deliver a complete set of the dishes with it, whether all were used or not. This way the next cook will have all the dishes she or he needs.

- As you plan the upcoming weeks, if you know you will be out of town, the others in the group can decide either to swap just between the two of them, find a substitute, or take the week off. Again, how this is works out is very individualized.

- Most of all, have fun! Happy eating.

Notes

Chapter Five—A Mom's Greatest Joy
1. C.S. Lewis, *The Lion, the Witch and the Wardrobe* (New York, NY: HarperCollins, 1950), p.164.

Chapter Eleven—Super Mom vs. Slacker Mom
1. Marilyn Heins, "Overparenting," <www.parentkidsright.com/pt-overparenting.html> On her website, Dr. Heins provides busy parents with commonsense advice, parenting skills, and strategies for everyday child raising through ParenTips and other features.
2. Victoria Clayton, "Overparenting," <www.msnbc.msn.com/id/6620793/-55k>
3. Kim Painter, "Moms Swing from Super to 'Slacker,'" <www.usatoday.com/life/books/news/2004-05-04-slacker-mom_x.htm>

Chapter Twelve—Boundaries, Please
1. This quote came from John Rosemond's website, which is full of great advice and helpful encouragement (see www.rosemond.com).

Chapter Fifteen—How in the World Do You Do What You Do?
1. Jan Johnson, *Living a Purpose-Full Life* (Colorado Springs, CO: Waterbrook Press, 1999), pp. 179-80, 186.

Chapter Seventeen—The Most Beautiful Scars
1. Wilfred A. Peterson, "The Art of Giving," as quoted in Jean Fleming, *A Mother's Heart* (Colorado Springs, CO: NavPress, 1982), p. 54.

Chapter Nineteen—Does Anyone Notice Me?
1. Angela Thomas Guffey, *Tender Mercy for a Mother's Soul* (Wheaton, IL: Tyndale House Publishers, 2001), p. 48.

Chapter Twenty-Two—Do They See Jesus in Me?
Epigraph: Tim Kimmel, *Why Christian Kids Rebel* (Nashville, TN: W Publishing Group, 2004) p. 91.
1. Ibid.

Chapter 23—Chasing Rainbows
1. Katharine C. Kersey, *The Art of Sensitive Parenting* (Herndon, VA: Acropolis Books, 1983).

Chapter 24—Remember to Look Up
1. *Life Application Bible NIV,* (Wheaton, IL, Tyndale House Publishers, 1988), commentary on p. 2153.

About the Author

Lysa TerKeurst is a wife, mother of five, and the president of Proverbs 31 Ministries. She is a frequent guest on *The 700 Club* and has appeared on many national programs, including *Focus on the Family* and *Good Morning America*. She has also been featured in *Family Circle* and *O, the Oprah* magazines.

The coauthor of *A Woman's Secret to a Balanced Life*, Lysa is also the author of *What Happens When Women Walk in Faith; Radically Obedient, Radically Blessed; Who Holds the Key to Your Heart?;* and *Capture His Heart.*

Please check out Proverbs 31 at www.proverbs31.org. You may contact Lysa via that website or by writing to:

Proverbs 31 Ministries
Attn.: Lysa TerKeurst
616-G Matthews-Mint Hill Road
Matthews, NC 28105

Lysa is also a nationally known speaker. For more information on booking her for an event, please contact LeAnn Rice at 704/849-2270.